C000154682

ISBN 978-0-267-62936-7
PIBN 10030441

FB &c Ltd, Dalton House, 60 Windsor Avenue, London, SW19 2RR.
Company number 08720141. Registered in England and Wales.

For support please visit www.forgottenbooks.com

A STRIKE
MADE BY

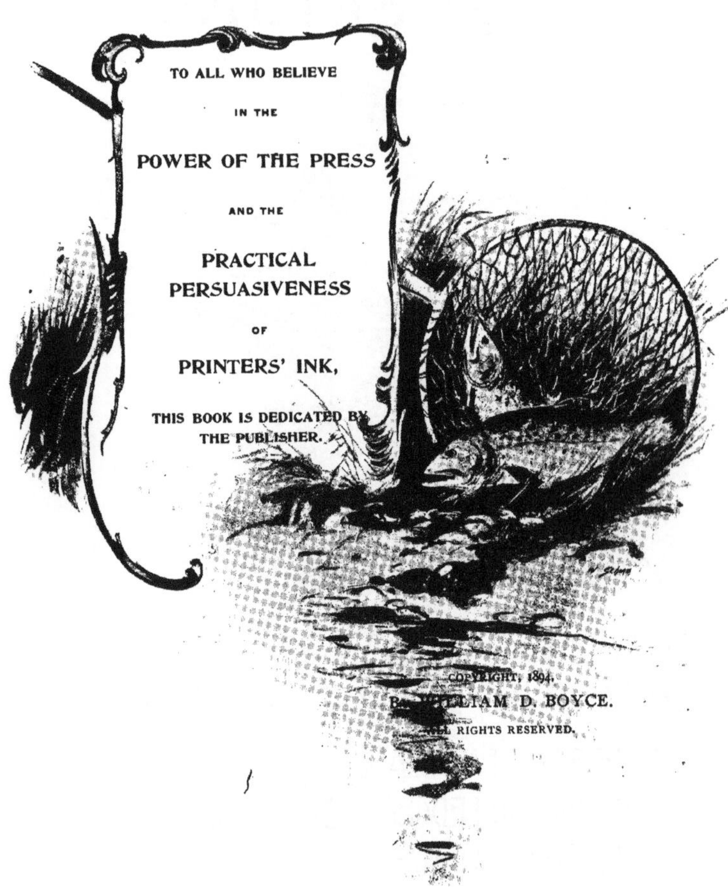

The Lakeside Press
R. R. DONNELLEY & SONS CO., CHICAGO

INTRODUCTION.

A glance at the presentation page will reveal the fact that the publisher has not issued this volume for revenue only, nor for protection, but principally for the good of the fraternity. Close inspection of the tints and texts of the turning leaves, which have been pressed into use for better preservation, may prove most pleasant and profitable to the reader; pleasant because the artistic illustrations bring to mind pictures of free out-door recreation, and profitable because business may be increased by adopting the suggestions made so plain that "even he who runs may read."

It was one of the modern philosophers who asserted that "nothing succeeds like success," and judged by this standard the publisher and presenter of the present volume is truly a successful man. He flourishes a BLADE more popular and powerful than the ancient "blade of Damascus," and no publisher of the present day can show a brighter or better LEDGER than the one which comes from his office. Mr. Boyce might not be willing to stand forth and make this just claim in his own behalf, but the editor of this work merely admits a well-known fact and violates no confidence in disclosing this open secret to all the world and the rest of mankind.

Having given credit to whom credit is due in this respect, the writer hastens to acknowledge his obligations to several of the standard authorities on American field sports and fishing for material aid in preparing this volume. To Isaac McLellan, the poet-sportsman, due credit should be given for most of the stanzas introducing the various descriptive sketches of the game fishes, animals and birds of the United States. These poetical selections are, for the most part, taken from McLellan's excellent "Poems of the Rod and Gun," a book of rare interest to anglers and sportsmen.

The well-known treatise, entitled "American Game Fishes," and the practical book, "Fishes of the East Atlantic Coast," by Messrs. Louis O. Van Doren and Samuel C. Clarke, veteran anglers, have likewise furnished valuable matter, for which proper acknowledgment has been made elsewhere under the several heads or chapters where the writers above named are quoted.

In the arrangement of the subject-matter the writer has been guided principally by the directions of the publisher—whose instructions to author, artist and printer, were to spare neither time, labor or expense in the preparation of a book to grace the library of the sportsman, the angler and the man of business.

It has been the belief of Mr. W. D. Boyce that a valuable work of reference, combining the information hitherto attainable only by possession of a sporting library, could be produced in attractive form, for the benefit of busy men who have neither time nor inclination to make extensive research for such facts.

The "Fish Tales" and "Hunters' Yarns," taken in moderation, with spirited illustrations, *ad lib.*, may serve as a prescription to drive away the blues. Such, at least, is the design of the publisher and his fellow conspirator—F. E. Pond.

PUBLISHER'S NOTE.

In the compiling and publishing of this little work I wish to acknowledge the valuable services of Fred E. Pond, (Will Wildwood) the Secretary of the National Game and Fish Protective Association of the United States, who compiled, under my direction, the matter herein contained. Also that of Wm. H. Schmedtgen, the well-known artist, whose work herein speaks for itself and will be praised by all who see it. The composition, make-up, press-work and binding has been done by my valued friend and former partner, Mr. R. R. Donnelley, who stands as the leading artist-printer in Chicago.

The true cause for the publication of this book is to afford us an opportunity to compliment our friends and show them that we will not allow them to forget us. Truly,

W. D. Boyce.

CONTENTS.

"THREE OF A KIND."

It is said that the fisherman, general advertiser and newspaper man are "three of a kind." This I have always been told beats "two pair." The reason, however, I understand, they are entered in the same class, is not so much because they do not always stick to the truth, but because they are not always believed.

Seriously, there is a great deal of the same makeup in the true sportsman and angler, plucky advertiser and hustling newspaper man. The fisherman must often wait and make many casts before he gets "a strike"—the general advertiser often casts his bread upon the waters for years before it returns to him one hundred fold—the publisher must keep everlastingly hustling or sink out of sight. Long waiting and patience is a necessary characteristic of the "three of a kind." Quick results are secured by advertising in *Boyce's Big Weeklies.*

REMARKS ON ANGLING.

"A taper rod, a slender line,
A bait to tempt the fishes,
And in the shade of oak or pine
One may the wicked world resign
And all its sinful wishes."

"A gamy fight, a landed prize,
Perhaps a bass to mention,
And tho' the world may advertise
'Twill never out of art devise
A parallel invention."

"O wearied souls that sigh for peace
And search the town, e'er failing,
Here is unwatered bliss to lease,
With interest beginning to increase —
And 'sou'west' winds prevailing."

Angling is probably the most ancient of out-door recreations. In the Apostolic days Peter said "I go a-fishing," and his brother disciples responded, "we also, will go with thee." Before the dawn of the Christian era angling was enjoyed as a pastime, though it had not developed into a profound science. When the Divine hand brought order out of chaos, created the earth, and appointed to the surface three-fourths water and one-fourth of dry land, the relative importance of fishing as compared with the sports of the field, was forever fixed and can scarcely be questioned. It has been said in favor of angling that "it is a one-handed game, that would have suited Adam himself; it is the onlyone by which Noah could have amused himself in the ark," and these truths seem self-evident.

Of ancient angling, as practiced by the Egyptians, the Assyrians, the Romans, and other races of ye olden time, little need be said in this volume. It may be safely assumed that the majority of fishers in that past age fished for food, not for pleasure. The angling appliances of the ancients were so crude and coarse—as evidenced by the relics of this kind preserved in various museums—that it would be ridiculous to term their method of fishing a "gentle art." Sinews and strings of raw-hide were the ordinary fishing lines, and the hooks were roughly formed of bone or metal. Respect for the reputation of the good and great men who inhabited the earth when it was comparatively new, prevents modern authors on angling from entertaining a belief that the fishes of old were caught "by main strength and ignorance," and the same reverence for antiquity will of course banish the satirical definition of old-time angling as "a stick and a string, with a fish at one end and a fool at the other." The writer will venture the statement, however, that the anglers of ancient days carried more live, natural flies than artificial ones during their fishing excursions.

In the legends and lyrics preserved—*cum grano salis*—from the past, references are made to mighty mythical anglers, worthy of a place at the camp fire or in the club rooms of the modern association of Angling Ananiases. Of one of those old worthies it was said:

> "He baited his hook with dragons' tails,
> And sat on a rock and bobbed for whales."

It is a pleasure to turn from the famous and the fabulous fishers of the dim past, to the anglers and angling of a more recent period. Foremost in the literature of angling stands that quaint and pleasing volume, "The Compleat Angler," written by Izaak Walton, whose tercentenary was celebrated quietly and appropriately, August 9, 1893, at the Walton Cottage—a unique building, modeled after his famous fishing lodge on the River Dove—and it is worthy of note that the great fly-casting tournament, held September 21, 1893, within the enclosure of the World's Columbian Exposition, was contested on the lagoon in front of the same cosy cot which had been erected there in honor of the world-renowned angler and author.

It is a singular fact, though entirely in harmony with the eternal fitness of things, that the earliest published treatise on the gentle art of angling was written by one of the gentle sex, Dame Juliana Berners, whose "Treatyse of Fysshynge wyth an Angle," issued in the year 1496, antedated the work of our beloved Izaak more than one hundred and fifty years. The instructions given by the venerable Dame are more curious than concise or correct, as applied to the wants of scientific devotees of rod and reel in the nineteenth century, but it must be borne in mind that America had not been discovered when Juliana Berners wrote her book, and the lady, although celebrated for her learning and accomplishments, had not the gift of prophecy to foretell of fish and fishing in the (then) unknown but now "Universal Yankee Nation."

Although the precepts of the quaint treatise appear antiquated and amusing to a degree, nearly all devoted lovers of angling will heartily agree with the feminine philosophy embodied in the statement that many miseries attend the sports of hunting, hawking, and fowling, and "dowteles therne folowyth it, that it must nedes be the dysporte of fysshynge wyth an angle that causeth a long lyfe and a mery." The conclusion thus drawn may not be satisfactory, nor the reasons clear to a field sportsman, but they are ample for the angling brotherhood.

Following down the line of famous English authors, from the days of Walton to the present time, it will be found that most of the immortals have published pleasant words relating to fishing as a pastime, and Sir Humphrey Davy gave to the world evidence of his love for the theme by writing that admirable work, "Salmonia, or Days of Fly Fishing;" while Prof. John Wilson (the inimitable "Christopher North") in his *Noctes Ambrosianae*, recorded some of the most attractive observations on angling in the whole range of modern literature.

In America several prominent literary men of the past half century have delighted the fishing fraternity with angling books and essays. Dr. Geo. W. Bethune, the great divine, found time amid his more serious labors, to prepare an elaborate American edition of Walton's Complete Angler, and Hon. Robert B. Roosevelt, diplomat and scholar, has written several volumes on fishing as entertaining and instructive in their way as are the thrilling works by his nephew,—the gifted Theodore Roosevelt—descriptive of the wild sports of the West. The well-earned fame of Charles Lanman rests equally upon his achievements as artist and angling author; while Henry William Herbert, the classical scholar and novelist, is best remembered under the name of "Frank Forester," his works on fishing and field sports taking high rank at the present day, though his historical romances, upon which he believed his literary reputation must depend, are nearly forgotten by the reading public.

It is evident that a pastime which holds the attention and warm admiration of scholarly men must have much to commend—much that "passeth the understanding" of those who have never felt the desire to go a-fishing. The familiar adage, "spare the rod and spoil the child," has been misunderstood and the rod misapplied for many generations past. The proper rod for the youth, in most cases, is not the birch but the bamboo, and this should be gently placed in the hand of the young student, with judicious instructions as to the best times and places for conning his new lines, concluding with the injunction that he must never allow his fly book to cause neglect of his school books.

Many born anglers have been driven almost to desperation, their minds and bodies suffering from the aforesaid misapplication of the rule and the rod. Give the schoolboy a good hook and line and rod, with occasional holidays for their use, and if he is of the right sort he will not "play hookey," nor will he miss his lines, or require the use of the rod in the school room. If parents and pedagogues would learn that there are times in the training of boys when a rod in the hand is worth two on the back, and that there are valuable lessons in the running brooks as well as in books, the world would be better and brighter.

Recreation is not merely amusement and relief from toil. In its best form—as for example, in angling—recreation literally re-creates both mind and body; mental troubles vanish and bodily ills mysteriously depart under the soothing influence of the forest shade and the pleasant song of the brook. Nature is the true healer, and the fishing rod is a magic wand to be waved over the waters, for mortal man will never come nearer the perennial Fountain of Youth than when he stands upon the brink of some crystal trout pool, or close to a circling eddy, where the salmon leaps.

Any angler can vouch for the fact that it is not all of fishing to fish. The alternate effects of sun and shade, the sights and sounds along sylvan shores, the balmy breeze, the odors of pine and balsam and the wild flowers of the wilderness—all these and a thousand other things only incidentally connected with fishing bring health and happiness to the ardent angler. In the words of Sir Egerton Brydges:

"It is a mingled rapture, and we find
The bodily spirit mounting to the mind."

No other out-door pastime is so free from noise, turmoil and confusion; so calm and peaceful, in the intervals or interludes of the play—the periods between expectation and realization—when the chirp of the cricket and the carol of birds relieve rather than break the silence, and the angler rejoices in moments of meditation, or quietly communes with the silent voices of Nature. In his pleasant ballad entitled The Angler's Song, quaint old Iz. Wa.—as he signs himself at the end of the Epistle Dedicatory of the "Compleat Angler"—the charm of fishing as a contemplative pastime is thus set forth:

Of recreation there is none
So free as fishing is alone;
All other pastimes do no less
Than mind and body both possess;
  My hand alone my work can do,
  So I can fish and study too.

In an entertaining essay on the pleasures of angling, the late "Harry Fernwood" gave the following comments on the theory and practice: "And so these men, whose teachings I would emulate, wore away their days tranquilly into the nineties. They saw their fellows pursuing intangible spectres—the curse of avarice, and the sham happiness of wealth, under which, in the heyday of manhood, they sank out of sight and recollection. Not that it is folly to get riches. The acquirement of fortune is all very well if not taken in exchange for health, which is at all odds the greatest of riches, of comforts, and of blessings. * * * The human system is like a bow, which, in order to preserve the tension, must be relaxed occasionally, and which becomes a worthless thing when its elasticity is no longer apparent.

"Why should Dame Juliana Berners write a work on angling? Because she found a charm in it. Nor is she wanting in admirers of her sex these five centuries past. On all my jaunts I meet the fairer patrons of the craft. And proper it is for them—far better for their future health than to become, like their fashionable sisters, listless, wan and flounced for show, dozing away the genial warmth of a summer day, invoking the 'tedious' hours on speed, and then to vex with mirth the drowsy ear of night, toying with fan and ammoniacal salts to coax the senses back.

"'To me more dear, congenial to my heart,
One native charm, than all the gloss of art.'"

"When fatigued and worn by the cares of a sedentary profession I have stolen away from the sultry town to some clear lake or stream, where the dandelion flecked the new-made green, and the blossomed orchards were fair to see. The sweet notes of the first birds of spring have cheered me on the way, and my line has gently rippled the glassy pool ere yet the blue smoke was curling from the cottage tops. I have known the struggle with the wiry *genii* of the stream, the sensations which thrilled my every nerve when the hook was seized. The fears of losing the fish, and the hope of safely landing him a prey to artful skill—the quietude of mind and rest of body I have experienced in a day so spent, have altogether made me equal to many an exigency of the daily task. And that is why I am an angler."

William T. Porter, familiarly known as "York's Tall Son," (the editor and founder of the first sportsman's journal in America,) published many years ago a series of descriptive essays on angling, his favorite pastime. The following extracts are taken from the sketches, which originally appeared in that rare and brilliant periodical, Porter's old *Spirit of the Times*:

"Fly-fishing has been designated the royal and aristocratic branch of the angler's craft, and unquestionably it is the most difficult, the most elegant, and to men of taste, by myriads of degrees, the most exciting and pleasant mode of angling. To land a trout of three, four, or five pounds weight, and sometimes heavier, with a hook almost invisible, with a gut line as delicate and beautiful as a single hair from the raven tresses of a mountain sylph, and with a rod not heavier than a tandem whip, is an achievement requiring no little presence of mind, united to consummate skill. If it be not so, and if it does not give you some very pretty palpitations of the heart in the performance, may we never wet a line in Lake George, or raise a trout in the Susquehanna. Fly-fishing requires many natural attributes, among which must chiefly be enumerated, a light and flexible hand and arm, a quick eye, and one that can 'squint straight,' caution, coolness, and an extreme delicacy of touch."

"From the sources of the Delaware and the Susquehanna to those of the Kennebec, and in the thousand mountain streams flowing into the St. Lawrence, trout fishing may now be enjoyed (May and June) in the utmost perfection. We have dreamed, or have somewhere heard, that it is not until the cowslip has shed its golden smiles over the meadows, and your ears are saluted with the vernal notes of the reed-sparrow; when the 'ephemera' or May-fly is seen (courting its destruction) giddily to wanton over the surface of the stream which only a few hours before brought it into existence, that trout are 'initiated into condition,' and rise freely to the fly. You may see them lurking in every direction in the ponds of New England; while on Long Island, he that cannot kill a few brace at the close of a summer afternoon, or before the sun gets up, should not be allowed to wet a line."

"The gray and green drake, which nearest resemble the May-fly, succeed it in their season, and are equally welcomed by 'Johnny Trout.' The *palmer* family follow in order, and may be used throughout the season with success. But there is, during the still evening of mid-summer, a minute black gnat, which riots in myriads over every stream, and we have seen trout in a continual state of excitement for above an hour in carping at these gnats. We confess our entire disbelief in a doctrine considered orthodox by many, that each season and stream has its peculiar and appropriate flies; and we have arrived at this conclusion after as much practical experience as many Waltonians who have attained the age of four-score. Since we were stout enough to wield a rod, our constant custom of an afternoon has been to put it to use, if, by hook or crook, we could; for which propensity many is the birchen one we have had applied to our shoulders, and we are free to say, that our experience goes to prove that with three flies well matched, there is very little necessity of cumbering one's hook with an infinite variety. Give us a red or brown hackle for the end of our leader, with a black midge for the first dropper, and a light salmon-colored butterfly not larger than your thumb-nail for the second, and we can raise from his cool retreat the craftiest trout that ever gorged a grasshopper, or turned up his nose in scorn at the bungling efforts of a greenhorn." Since angling has become the chosen recreation of presidents, poets, and parsons, the charming essay which appeared long ago in one of the prominent literary periodicals of New York City, over the signature of Henry Ward Beecher, will serve well to round out the chapter of remarks on angling. The sketch referred to was published under the title of

TROUTING.

Where shall we go? Here is the Mare brook, the upper part running through bushy and wet meadows, but the lower part flowing transparently over the gravel, through the grass and pasture grounds near the edge of the village, where it curves and winds and ties itself into bow knots. It is a charming brook to catch trout in, when you can catch them, but they are mostly caught.

Well, there is the Candy brook. We will look at that. A man might walk through the meadows and not suspect its existence. The grass meets over the top of its upper section, and quite hides it; and below, through that iron-tinctured marsh land, it expands only a little, growing open-hearted by degrees, across a narrow field; and then it runs for the thickets—and he that takes fish among those alders will certainly earn

A taper rod, a slender line,
A bait to tempt the fishes,
And in the shade of oak or pine
One may the wicked world resign
And all its sinful wishes.

GEO. F. BOWEN.

them. Yet, for its length, it is not a bad brook. The trout are not numerous, nor large, nor especially fine, but every one you catch renews your surprise that you should catch *any* in such a ribbon of a brook. Still farther north is another stream, something larger, and much better or worse, according to your luck. It is easy of access, and quite unpretending. There is a bit of a pond, some twenty feet in diameter, from which it flows, and in that there are five or six half-pound trout, who seem to have retired from active life and given themselves to meditation in this liquid convent. They were very tempting but quite untemptable. Standing afar off we selected an irresistible fly, and with long line we sent it pat into the very place. No trout should have hesitated a moment. The morsel was delicious. The nimblest of them should have flashed through the water, broke the surface, and with a graceful but decisive curve plunged downward, carrying the insect with him. Then we should in our turn very cheerfully lend him a hand, relieve him of his prey, and admiring his beauty, but pitying his untimely fate, buried him in the basket. But he wished no translation. We cast our fly again and again; we drew it hither and thither; we made it skip and wriggle; we let it fall plash like a surprised miller; and our audience calmly beheld our feats.

Next we tried ground bait, and sent our vermicular hook down to their very sides. With judicious gravity they parted, and slowly sailed toward the root of an old tree on the side of the pool. Again changing place, we will make an ambassador of a grasshopper. Laying down our rod, we prepare to catch the grasshopper; that is in itself no slight feat. The first step you take at least forty bolt out, and tumble headlong in the grass; some cling to the stems, some are creeping under the leaves, and not one seems to be in reach. You step again; another flight takes place, and you eye them with a fierce penetration, as if you could catch some one with your eye. You cannot, though. You brush the grass with your foot again. Another hundred snap out, and tumble about in every direction. At length you see a very nice young fellow climbing a steeple stem. You take good aim and grab at him. You catch the spire, but he has jumped a safe rod. Yonder is another, creeping among some delicate ferns. With broad palm you clutch him and all the neighboring herbage too. Stealthily opening your little finger, you see his leg; the next finger reveals more of him; and opening the next you are just beginning to take him out with the other hand, when out he bounds and leaves you to renew your entomological pursuits. Twice you snatch handfulls of grass, and cautiously open your palm to find that you have only grass. It is quite vexatious. There are thousands of them here and there, climbing and wriggling on that blade, leaping off from that stalk, twisting and kicking on that vertical spider's web, jumping and bounding about under your very nose, hitting you in your face, creeping on your shoes, and yet not one do you get. If any tender-hearted person ever wondered how a humane man could bring himself to such cruelty as to impale an insect, let him hunt for a grasshopper in a hot day among tall grass, and when at length he secures one, the affixing him upon the hook will be done without a single scruple, and as a mere matter of penal justice, and with judicial solemnity.

Now then the trout are yonder. We swing our line to the air, and give it a gentle cast toward the desired spot, and a puff of south wind dexterously lodges it in the branch of a tree. You plainly see it strike, and whirl over and over, so that no gentle pull loosens it; you draw it north and south, east and west; you give it a jerk up and a pull down; you give it a series of nimble twitches; you coax it in this way, and solicit it in that way, in vain. Then you stop and look a moment, first at the trout, and then at your line. Was there anything ever so vexatious? Would it be wrong to get angry? In fact you feel very much like it. The very things you wanted to catch, the grasshopper and the trout, you could not; but a tree, that you did not want, you have caught fast at the first throw. You fear that the trout will be scared. You cautiously draw nigh and peep down. Yes, there they are looking at you, and laughing as sure as ever trout laughed. They understand the whole thing. With a very decisive jerk you snap your line, regain the remnant of it, and sit down to repair it, to put on another hook, catch another grasshopper, and move on down stream to catch a trout.

But let us begin. Standing in the middle of the stream, your short rod in hand, let out twelve to twenty feet of line, varying its length according to the nature of the stream, and, as far as it can be done, keeping its position and general conduct under anxious scrutiny. Just here the water is mid-leg deep. Experimenting at each forward reach for a firm foot-hold, slipping, stumbling over some uncouth stone, slipping on the moss of another, reeling and staggering, you will have a fine opportunity of testing the old philosophical dictum, that you can think of but one thing at a time. You must think of half a dozen; of your feet, or you will be sprawling in the brook; of your eyes and face, or the branches will scratch them; of your line, or it will tangle at every step; of your far-distant hook and dimly seen bait, or you will lose the end of all your fishing. At first it is a puzzling business. A little practice sets things all right.

Do you see that reach of shallow water gathered to a head by a cross-bar of sunken rocks? The water splits in going over upon a slab of rock below, and forms an eddy to the right and one to the left. Let us try a grasshopper there. Casting it in above, and guiding it by a motion of your rod, over it goes, and whirls out of the myriad bubbles into the edge of the eddy, when, quick as a wink, the water breaks open, a tail flashes in the air and disappears, but re-appears to the instant backward motion of your hand, and the victim comes skittering up the stream, whirling over and over, till your hand grasps him, extricates the hook, and slips him into the basket. Poor fellow! you *want* to be sorry for him, but every time you try you are glad instead. Standing still, you bait again, and try the other side of the stream, where the water, wiping off the bubbles from its face, is taking toward that deep spot under a side rock. There! you've got him! Still tempting these two shores, you take five in all, and then the tribes below grow cautious. Letting your line run before you, you wade along, holding on by this branch, fumbling with your feet along the jagged channel, changing hands to a bough on the left side, leaning on that rock, stepping over that stranded log. Ripping a generous hole in your skirt as you leave it, you come to the edge of the petty fall. You step down, thinking only how to keep your balance, and not at all of the probable depth of water, till you splash and plunge down into a basin waist-deep. The first sensation of a man up to his vest pockets in water, is peculiarly foolish, and his first laugh rather faint; and he is afterward a little ashamed of the alacrity with which he scrambles for the bank. A step or two brings you to a sand-bank and to yourself. But while you are in a scrape at one end of your line, a trout has got into a worse one at the other. A little flurried with surprise at both experiences, you come near losing him in the injudicious haste with which you overhaul him.

GAME FISHES

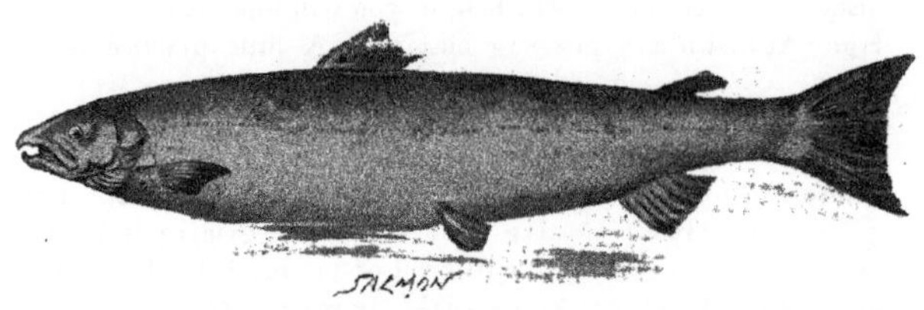

> "Cold, those rivers, as the fountains
> From the wilderness that flow,
> Cold as waters of the mountains,
> Gelid with the ice and snow,
> There amid the soft abysses,
> Or the river's spring-fresh tide,
> Gleaming, flashing, leaping, diving,
> Shoals of lordly salmon glide."

The salmon family is considered the royal branch in tracing the various species of game fish in American waters, and the sea salmon is undisputed king in this line. It is not solely on account of size that the salmon holds this honored position, for the mascalonge would prove a formidable rival in this respect, but it is the combination of game qualities, and particularly that of rising to the artificial fly and fighting for liberty when hooked, with wonderful strength, activity and sagacity, making the result doubtful to the last, that gives such zest to salmon fishing.

Although the salmon takes an annual outing, so to speak, in the ocean waves, it is practically a fresh water fish from the angler's point of view, as it is born in the clear cold rivers flowing to the sea, and returns each season to the vicinity of its birth place, by instinct as unerring as that of the carrier pigeon. No ordinary obstacle will stop the fish when ascending his native river, and remarkable incidents are told illustrating the endurance, perseverance and acrobatic powers of the salmon in overcoming the natural and artificial barriers of the stream.

It is now believed by our leading naturalists that "the original habitat of the entire family *Salmonidæ* was in fresh water, and that it is the sea salmon which has become erratic—the disturbances of the glacial period having driven them out of their primitive inland possessions. But in obedience to the law of evolution which requires posterity to pass through the same biological changes as their progenitors did, all salmon must be born and live for a time, at least, in fresh water; hence we find our sea salmon coming into the rivers and spending a large proportion of their time in fresh water, seeking there a change of diet and hygienic treatment against parasites and fungus." These observations, from the pen of a practical angler-naturalist, appear reasonable and forcible.

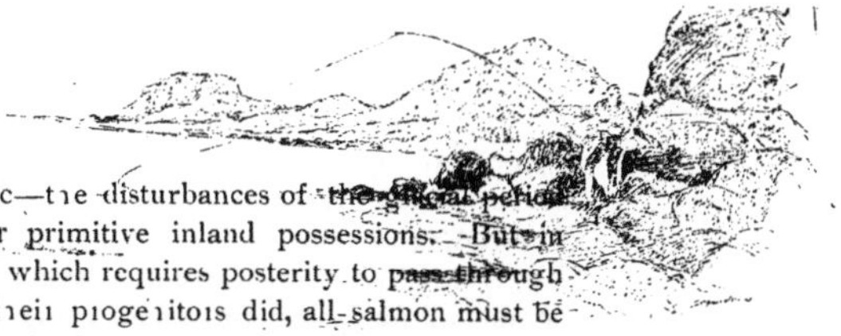

The Atlantic salmon—considered the best game fish of the several closely allied species—is described as follows by scientists, as to appearance and general characteristics: Body moderately elongate, symmetrical, not generally compressed. Head rather low. Mouth moderate, the maxillary reaching just past the eye. Scales rather large, largest posteriorly, and silvery in appearance. Coloration in the adult brownish above, the sides more or less silvery, with numerous black spots on sides of head, on body, and on fins, and red patches along the sides in the males; young specimens (parrs) with about eleven dusky cross-bars, besides black spots and red patches, the color, as well as form of the head and body varying much with age, food and condition; the black spots in the adult often x shaped, or x x shaped. Weight fifteen to forty pounds. North Atlantic, ascending all suitable rivers and the region north of Cape Cod; sometimes permanently land-locked in lakes, where its habits and colorations (but no tangible specific characters) changed somewhat when it becomes, in America, var. *Sebago*.

Salmon fishing is beyond doubt royal sport, and under present conditions it cannot be enjoyed to the full extent by any American anglers except those having royal incomes, as the Canadian tour, cost of fishing lease, guide, boatman, etc., bring the expense well up in round numbers, making the ordinary "silver lure" burdensome, good gold eagles being preferable for the line of rapid transit. In the early portion of the past century the Hudson river was a magnificent salmon stream, but the changes wrought by time and the tide of commerce have so fettered it and polluted the natural tide that it now leads to fortune more than to fishing. The head waters of the Hudson have of late been restocked, and a number of salmon of moderate size were taken last season below an impassable dam, thus proving that if suitable fish-ways can be secured, and necessary restrictions against seining put into effect, the river will again furnish excellent sport for salmon fishers. Much credit is due to Mr. A. N. Cheney, of Glens Falls, N. Y., for organizing a strong association to promote the good work of restoring the salmon fishing of the Hudson.

If properly supported success will be assured, and the movement will be of incalculable value to the state whether considered from an angling or a financial standpoint.

A few rivers in Maine and several streams along the Pacific coast afford fair fly-fishing for salmon, but the large majority of American anglers, seeking for sport in this line, visit the streams tributary to the St. Lawrence, where the fishing exploits of such past masters of the craft as Dr. Bethune, "Frank Forester," Robert B. Roosevelt, Charles Lanman, Charles Hallock, and a host of other worthies, have drawn public attention to the exclusion, almost, of minor resorts. Let us hope the day is not far distant when our own rivers, judiciously restocked and protected, will furnish fishing equally good for the recreation of our anglers.

It would be folly to attempt instruction, even as to the first principles of practical salmon fishing, in a few pages devoted to this subject. So far as primary lessons can be given in entertaining and instructive form, the reader is commended to a careful perusal of Chas. Hallock's admirable book, "The Salmon Fisher," and Henry P. Wells' "American Salmon Fisherman"—two volumes full of interest and instruction for students preparing to take the coveted degree of master of arts in the school of angling.

Mr. George Dawson, in his captivating work, entitled "Pleasures of Angling," gives a realistic description of the sensations he experienced in catching his first salmon. After securing a rise, and gazing upon the fish, face to face; beholding the cavernous mouth and bulging eyes of his finny adversary, just rising from the depths, the angler experienced the feeling of faintness, followed by electric thrills usual at this stage; and then, exerting every effort to regain composure, he made a second cast.

The story is best told in his own words: "I had marked the spot where the fish had risen, had gathered up my line for another cast, had dropped the fly, like a snow-flake, just where I desired it to rest, when, like a flash, the same enormous head appeared, the same open jaws revealed themselves, a swirl and a leap and a strike followed, and the salmon was hooked with a thud! which told me as plainly as if the operation had transpired within the range of my vision, that if I lost him it would be my own fault. When thus assured, there was excitement, but no flurry. My nerves thrilled and every muscle assumed the tension of well-tempered steel, but I realized the full sublimity of the occasion, and a sort of majestic calmness took the place of the stupid-inaction which followed the first apparition. My untested rod bent under the pressure in a graceful curve; my reel clicked out a livelier melody than ever emanated from harp or hautboy, as the astonished fish made his first dash; the tensioned line emitted Æolian music as it stretched and stiffened under the strain to which it was subjected; and for fifty minutes there was such giving and taking, such sulking and rushing, such leaping and tearing, such roping and fearing, as would have 'injected life into the ribs of death,' made an anchorite dance in very ecstasy, and caused any true angler to believe that his heart was a kettle-drum, every sinew a jew's-harp, and the whole frame-work of his excited nerves a full band of music. And during all this time my canoe-man rendered efficient service in keeping even pace with the eccentric movements of the struggling fish. 'Hold him head up, if possible!' was the counsel given me, and 'make him work for every inch of line.' Whether, therefore, he took fifty yards or a foot, I tried to make him pull for it, and then to regain whatever was taken as soon as possible. The result was an incessant clicking of the reel, either in paying out or in taking in, with an occasional flurry and leap which could have been no more prevented than the onrushing of a locomotive. Any attempt to have suddenly checked him by making adequate resistance would have made leader, line or rod a wreck in an instant. All that it was proper or safe to do was to give each just the amount of strain and pressure it could bear with safety—not an ounce more nor an ounce less—and I believe that I measured the pressure so exactly that the strain upon my rod did not vary half an ounce from the first to the last of the struggle. Toward the close of the fight, when it was evident that the 'jig was up,' and I felt myself master of the situation, I took my stand upon a projecting point in the river, where the water was shallow, and where the most favorable opportunity possible was afforded the gaffer to give the struggling fish the final death thrust, and so end the battle. It was skillfully done. The first plunge of the gaff brought him to the greensward, and there lay out before me, in all his silver beauty and magnificent proportions, my first salmon. He weighed thirty pounds, measured nearly four feet in length, was killed in fifty minutes. It is said that when the good old Dr. Bethune landed *his* first salmon, 'he caressed it as fondly as he ever caressed his first born.' I could only stand over mine in speechless admiration and delight—panting with fatigue, trembling in very ecstasy."

Summing up his afterthoughts on this occasion, the author adds: "The victory was a surfeit for the morning. With other fish in full view, ready to give me a repetition of the grand sport I had already experienced, I made no other cast, and retired perfectly contented. The beautiful fish was laid down lovingly in the bottom of the canoe and borne in triumph to the camp, where fish and fisher were given such a hearty welcome amid such hilarious enthusiasm as was befitting 'the cause and the occasion.'" A thrilling incident, well written.

BROOK TROUT.

"Here, where the willowy thickets lave
Their drooping tassels beneath the wave,
There lies a deep and darkened pool
Whose waters are crystal clear and cool;
It is fed by many a gurgling fount
That trickles from upland pasture and mount,
And where the tree-shadows fall dense and dim
The glittering trout securely swim."

Of the brook trout—the justly prized 'salmon of the fountain'—it may truthfully be said that 'tis the popular favorite among most lovers of fly-fishing in the United States. Like the garnet the speckled trout sparkles for the multitude, while that gem of the first water, the salmon, gleams in its silvery lustre for the favored few. The brook trout is more widely distributed, and therefore more generally known than any other fresh water game fish of the first order, with the exception, possibly, of the black bass.

The natural habitat of the speckled trout is the section of country comprising the principal Eastern, New England and extreme Northern states, along the Canadian border, and westward to the sources of the Mississippi and those streams tributary to Lake Superior, where some of the largest specimens are found, ranking in size and game qualities with the magnificent trout of Maine waters. The southern range extends to the foot-hills of the Alleghanies, and the headwaters of the Chattahoochie, in Georgia, with a moderate number in the North Carolina tributaries of the Catawba. Many of the fish caught and recorded under the name of brook trout in certain sections of the United States, belong in reality to other species, and the local name, trout, is therefore a misnomer, frequently.

No other species of game fish varies so greatly in coloration and [illegible] the conditions of water and food acting upon the sensitive organism of the brook trout with effect almost equal to that of light and shade upon the changeful chameleon. In streams flowing over gravelly bottom and sandy soil, and through varied meadow-land and forest; or where the foot-hills of the mountains give dash and sparkle to the rivulets running down their slopes, the colors of the brook trout are brightest and the form of the fish most beautiful. In sluggish waters, dark and somber, shaded by heavy woodlands, the trout seem to belong to a different variety, hence the confusion existing in local names and nomenclature. An interesting and instructive exhibit might be made of genuine brook trout, taken from twenty widely separated localities, entirely unlike in character, and affording a family of fish apparently representing a score of species.

The majority of anglers are familiar, through personal experience or published description, with the carmine-dotted appearance of the brook trout. A volume would scarcely be sufficient to reveal the variety of colorings, characteristics and modes of capture. As well attempt to describe the shifting scenes of a kaleidoscope, or give a pen-picture of the varying tints and texture of the rainbow. The best method of studying the sprightly salmon of the fountain is not through merely reading the printed line, but consists rather in casting the silken line 'with neatness and despatch,' directly to his home. If the invitation is delicately sent and properly delivered the response will be prompt, and after overcoming the natural diffidence and reluctance of your new acquaintance, you may have the supreme satisfaction of placing him at your right hand—the position of honor—at your dining table.

The character of brook-trout fishing is as variable and fascinating as the coloration and habits of the fish. Fly-fishing is of course the highest and most enjoyable form of the art, though bait-fishing is by no means a tame or dull recreation. In fishing with the fly there is perhaps more of the picturesque, the artistic and scientific, but in bait-fishing a greater amount of energy, patience and perseverance may often be required. One well-known authority, Thomas Tod Stoddart, even declares that "worm-fishing for trout, when the waters are clear and low, the skies bright and warm, requires essentially more address and experience, as well as better knowledge of the habits and instincts of the fish, than fly-fishing." Leaving this debatable question aside, there is sufficient sport in either style of fishing to satisfy any except the most critical angler.

The trout-fisher at his best is one of the happiest of mortals. His lines are surely cast in pleasant places, along the cold spring brooks, where the mingled murmur of winds and woods and waters makes low music to his ears, the changeful scene affords a succession of pleasing pictures to the eye, and the velvet turf is like a carpet to the feet. Or his steps may wander near the foamy cataract, the deep river, and quiet lake, for the haunts of trout are found in a wide diversity of places. In the vicinity of Ashland, Wis., for instance, a long rocky ledge overhangs the shore of Chequamegon Bay, a short distance below the mouth of one of the favorite trout streams of that locality, and some of the largest specimens have been caught by a method known to the natives as "rock-fishing," which consists in fly-fishing from a boat carefully propelled along near shore, giving the angler opportunity to cast his line beneath the beetling crags where the lurking trout lie in wait.

The science of fly-casting — and it is certainly a scientific attainment — may be partially mastered by tournament methods and practice, but the critical test must be made at the trout-stream, where it will be found that the angler has ample use for all his resources of accuracy and delicacy, though he may usually dispense with the long distance cast that wins all the grand-stand applause. The Chicago Fly-Casting Club very properly gave precedence to points of delicate and accurate work, in summing up the respective merits of contestants at the World's Fair Tournaments, thus recognizing the most essential requirements for successful fly-fishing, particularly for brook-trout.

In his practical treatise entitled "Where the Trout Hide," the author, Kit Clarke, gives many excellent suggestions as to how, when and where to fish with the fly, and the book therefore furnishes a valuable lesson for the novice in trout-fishing. To the book and the brook the amateur may safely go for instruction.

There lies a deep and darkened pool
Whose waters are crystal clear and cool.

SMALL MOUTH BLACK BASS.
From Photograph.

WEIGHT, 6¼ LBS.
CAUGHT BY W. D. BOYCE,
AUGUST, 1894.

"In shallows of the river-reach
  Where rock and pebbles chafe the tide,
Where o'er white gravel and the sand
  The rushing waters foam and glide,
There oft the angler with his fly
  Takes the black rovers where they lie."

The above lines from the poet-sportsman, Isaac McLellan, run smoothly and bring to the mind a picture of black-bass fishing with the artificial fly. This bold game-fish, formerly little known and less prized by the majority of anglers, has within the past ten years been accorded its proper place in the first rank, by reason of the spirited essays and graphic descriptive sketches in the sportsmen's journals, and more particularly the excellent "Book of the Black Bass," from the pen of our modern apostle on this subject, Dr. James A. Henshall.

Two species of this distinctively American game fish, the large-mouthed black bass and the small-mouthed black bass, are found in the lakes and streams of the United States. The distinguishing features of the two, as described by the author previously quoted, may be easily observed, as "the angle of the mouth in the small-mouthed bass reaches only to, or below, the eye; while in the large-mouthed bass it extends considerably beyond, or behind it." He also adds that the angler who will bear in mind the difference thus: small mouth and small scales; large mouth and large scales, — will never be at a loss to identify the black bass species.

Great confusion exists, however, in various sections of the country regarding the black bass. In the south both species are generally miscalled "trout;" in portions of Kentucky it is known as the "jumping perch;" in North Carolina it appears as the "trout-perch" and "white salmon;" in Virginia it is termed the "chub," and in the Northern States, while the term bass is usually applied, some local appellation is frequently added, as "tiger bass," "buck bass," yellow or green bass, river, cove, lake, slough, or marsh bass, and in some instances Oswego bass.

It will be seen that the local names for the black bass are as varied as the geographical range of the two species, which extends to nearly every state east of the Rocky Mountains. In weight the small-mouthed bass ordinarily attains to about five pounds, and the large-mouthed seven pounds, as a maximum, though occasionally larger specimens have been taken of each kind, especially the latter species, which, in southern waters, sometimes reaches sixteen pounds. The colors of the black bass vary in different sections and even those caught in the same lake or stream show considerable variation, but the prevailing tinge is an olive-green, darkest on the back, lighter on the sides, and nearly white on the belly.

The favorite natural food of the bass consists of crawfish and minnows — the former preferred — though the various flies are seized with avidity, during the season when these appear over the surface of the waters. Black bass fishing on the inland lakes and rivers, whether with the natural bait or the artificial fly, is a most exhilarating pastime. Stream fishing is preferable for most anglers, as the methods employed — wading, or casting from the shore — give greater variety of scene and an opportunity for more exciting play, than lake fishing from a boat. Reef-fishing, about the Bass Islands of Lake Erie, which forms a distinct branch, differing in most respects from the ordinary bass-fishing, is enjoyed by many anglers who annually visit the resort, and catch large fish under the ledges, in water ten to twenty feet deep.

In fly-fishing a rod ten feet and three inches in length, and of seven and one half ounces weight is recommended by Dr. Henshall. The rod should be stiffer than one used for trout-fishing, as the bass are usually much larger than the brook trout; the reel a single-action click-reel; and the line an enameled, braided silk fly-line, with a carefully selected leader, about six feet long, and a moderate sized fly of brown, red, black, gray or ginger hackle.

The charm of this branch of angling is graphically described by Dr. Henshall, who remarks that in stream-fishing the angler "has the birds and flowers, the whispering leaves, the laughing water—old and genial friends of whom he never tires, whose fellowship is never wearisome, whose company is never dull. There are no harsh or discordant sounds on the stream—nothing to offend the eye or ear. Even the kingfisher's rattle, the caw of the crow, the tinkle of the cow-bell, the bark of the squirrel are softened and subdued and harmonized by the ripple of the stream and the rustle of the overhanging trees. All is joy and gladness, peace and contentment, by the merry shallows and quiet pools of the flowing, rushing stream. The swish of the rod, the hum of the reel, the cutting of the line through the water, the leap of the bass, seem somehow to blend with the voices of the stream and the trees on its banks, and to speak to the angler in louder, though sweeter, tones than on open waters; such sounds seem to be more intensified or heightened in their effect by some mysterious acoustic property of the stream and its surroundings. And the occasional 'pipe of peace' in some shady nook or sequestered spot, where, stretched at full length, the angler watches the nicotine incense assuming all manner of weird shapes as it ascends toward the tree-tops, while he indulges in fanciful day-dreams, with the cool breeze fanning his heated brow—the soft ferns resting his tired limbs! Yea, verily, this is the fishing beyond compare."

MASCALONGE.
From Photograph.

WEIGHT, 28 LBS.
CAUGHT BY W. D. BOYCE,
AUGUST, 1894.

"For earliest sport try the waters in May,
The mascalonge then will be leaping in play;
But better, by far, is the fishing in June,
When weirdly re-echoes the cry of the loon;
Or, if you prefer the sweet by and by,
Bring the rod and the reel in sultry July."

Chief among the members of the pike family is the mascalonge—a giant in size and a game fish of high order. In Canada and along the border line in the United States, the name "maskinonge" is much used, and the fish in the other sections is variously known as "muskallonge," "masquinongy," etc. The derivation of the name is from the French masque allonge ("long face"), the Chippewa term, "maskinonge," having similar meaning.

In size the mascalonge takes rank with the salmon, attaining a weight of from forty to fifty pounds, and Dr. E. Sterling records an instance of having speared one, nearly fifty years ago, weighing eighty pounds. Fish of this species weighing twenty pounds are quite common, and specimens of forty pounds weight are no rarity in suitable waters where fishing has been indulged in only to a moderate degree. As a means of identifying the mascalonge—which closely resembles the larger pike and pickerel in certain respects—an angling authority states that the difference may be easily detected by observing the gill covers. The lower half of cheek and gill-cover in the mascalonge are destitute of scales, while the pike has the cheek fully covered with scales, and in the pickerel it will be observed that both cheek and gill cover are grown with scales.

The range of this species is quite extensive, from the St. Lawrence in the East to the upper Mississippi in the West, and southward to the Tennessee River. It furnishes good sport to the angler, and as a food fish is superior to other members of the pike family. Trolling with live minnow or artificial bait is the favorite method of fishing for mascalonge, and when taken with a bass-rod the play is exciting. The fish, particularly in Wisconsin waters and in the St. Lawrence, leaps above the surface in the attempt to get free from the hook, and although much inferior to the salmon, whether as a game or food fish, it is one of the best of inland fishes. A live minnow or frog will prove a good lure in trolling or casting for mascalonge.

The admirers of the species have christened this fish "the tarpon of the North," and he is sometimes called the "tiger of the fresh waters," but under any title he is a valiant fighter, a bold, fierce biter, and worthy of the angler's attention in the lake or out of his native element, on the banquet board. Strong tackle and cool, skillful play are essential to success in capturing the large specimens, and a forty-pounder, after furnishing a royal battle for a half hour or more, will grace a hall or club-room excellently, if well mounted by a taxidermist.

THE SEA BASS.

"Wide off Long Island's yellow beach,
Where fisher's plummet scarce may reach,
Deep-sunken in the depths of brine,
Where sea-weeds all the rocks entwine,
Where kelp its beaded ribbon flings,
And the black mussel closely clings,
And sea-dulse their long tresses flaunt,
There the dark sea-bass makes his haunt."

Fresh from the water the sea-bass is considered a good food fish, but its flavor soon fails and becomes insipid. In like manner the resistance of the fish against capture consists in one weak flurry, when it yields tamely and comes to the surface like a dead weight.

In coloration the sea-bass is beautiful, being dark blue, with gills of scarlet tinge, the inside of mouth bright yellow, and the abdomen pale blue, with spots of various shades covering the body. The fins are large, and the body strong, though rather coarse in outline. The sea-bass is not abundant in northern waters, though it was in former years caught in large numbers along the coast of New York, New Jersey and Massachusetts. In weight the sea-bass runs from one pound to three pounds. It inhabits the deep water, is a bottom feeder, and is usually caught, in northern resorts, during October or early in November. The flood-tide is the best for sea-bass fishing, and sandworms and clams are favorite baits.

PIKE AND PICKEREL.

"By blue lake marge, upon whose breast
The water-lilies love to rest,
Lurking beneath those leaves of green
The fierce pike seeks his covert screen,
And thence with sudden plunge and leap,
Swift as a shaft through air may sweep.
He seizes, rends, and bears away
To hidden lair his struggling prey."

Pickerel-fishing is a sort of intermediate branch in the art of angling. It is a degree higher than perch or rock-bass fishing, and several degrees lower than trout and salmon fishing, in the estimation of skilled devotees of rod and line. The pike and pickerel, however, furnish sport for the multitudes of fishermen remote from the streams and lakes affording black bass, brook trout or salmon-fishing.

The habitat of these closely allied species of the pike family covers perhaps a wider geographical range than any other variety of fish worthy of classification under the head of American game fishes. They are found in most of the inland lakes and rivers, of the Eastern as well as the Western states, and nearly every man or boy familiar with any kind of fresh water fishing will recognize one or both of the species readily, although the confusion of fish lore is such that their identity is often as badly mixed as that of the two Dromios. To make "confusion worse confounded," the pike-perch is in many localities popularly supposed to be the true pike, and the genuine pike passes for pickerel. No one need err in identifying either of two last-named—i. e., pike and pickerel—if the simple test named in the article on the mascalonge be borne in mind.

It may not be generally known that pickerel will occasionally rise to the fly—though fly-fishing for this species would be a very uncertain and unsatisfactory sport. It is only an incidental by-play when fly-fishing for black bass, and under such circumstances will be found a novelty, interesting by way of variety. The pike, proper, will seldom, if ever, rise to the fly, but is a bold biter and will take the minnow, frog, trolling spoon, or other bait, in a ravenous manner, and furnish exciting play. The pike sometimes attains a weight of eighteen or twenty pounds, and in a few instances fish of this species have been taken weighing twenty-five pounds.

Professor Jordan describes the members of the pickerel family, five in number, thus: "Common Eastern pickerel (green pike); snout much prolonged, front of eye about midway in head; coloration green; sides with net-work of brown streaks; found in streams of Atlantic States.—Hump-backed pickerel, elevated back and broad, swollen ante-dorsal region; colors plain (olive green); found in Western States.—Banded pickerel or trout pickerel; snout much shorter than in preceding; eye nearer snout; color, dark green; sides, twenty blackish curved bars; rarely a foot long; home, Atlantic streams.—Little pickerel, or Western trout pickerel; size and form of preceding; more slender; color, olivaceous green above, tinting to white below; sides, curved streaks instead of bars; black streak in front of eye as well as below; abundant in Western streams."

WALL-EYED PIKE.

"The wall eyed pike so phantom-like
In waters clear and cold;
Its heavy strike like driven spike,
Its silvery scales and gold."

The pike-perch, more commonly known as the wall-eyed pike, is common in the Northern and Northwestern states, where the species is a popular favorite with boy-anglers, among whom the fish is regarded as a prize. The usual weight is from two to five pounds, but large specimens are sometimes taken weighing nearly thirty pounds. Although it is not considered a game-fish, of any special merit, the pike-perch is a food fish of better flavor and finer flesh than the ordinary pike and pickerel.

In still or sluggish waters the wall-eyed pike, when hooked, shows little activity and is not regarded with favor by anglers, but in swift streams the character of the fish is entirely different. It is usually taken either by still-fishing or trolling, the latter method, of course, giving the best sport. The fish are abundant in many Western lakes and streams, and as an edible fish it is held in deservedly high estimation.

The form of the pike-perch is comparatively slender and graceful, particularly in specimens of moderate size, and the general resemblance of the various species of the perch family can be readily traced in all, from the so-called 'wall-eyed pike' down to the common yellow perch familiar to almost every youthful angler. The local name of "wall-eye" is suggestive of the large staring eyes—perhaps the most noticeable feature of the pike-perch. On the sides the scales are usually of an old gold tinge, fading to silvery white beneath, furnishing a combination to satisfy any bi-metallic angler in this respect, whatever his opinion may be as to the game qualities of the fish.

THE GRAYLING.

"I wind about, and in and out,
With here a blossom sailing,
And here and there a lusty trout,
And here and there a grayling."

Among all the species of the finny tribe that furnish recreation for the angler, no other perhaps is so ethereal and dainty, so graceful in form, fin and outline, or so delicate in tints, as the grayling. In the waters of the United States—principally in the streams of Michigan—the rise and fall of the grayling has been remarkable, the species having risen rapidly in public estimation with a proportionate falling off in supply since angling writers first described and eulogised the American variety, about 1860.

The scientific name, *Thymallus*, applied to this species of the family Salmonidæ, has reference to the odor of thyme, so marked that in England the grayling is called "the flower of fishes." The Michigan variety seldom weighs more than a pound and a half, but the elegant form, the delicate shades of silver gray, olive brown and pale blue, and above all the magnificent dorsal fin, rising to the height of two inches, extending in its curved outline about one-fourth the length of the fish, and dotted like a waving banner with purple spots surrounded with greenish tints—combine to make the grayling a thing of beauty.

The great dorsal fin is the chief mark of loveliness, and the general appearance of the fish is thus described by a prominent ichthyologist: "The sun's rays, lighting up the delicate olive-brown tints of the back and sides, the bluish-white of the abdomen, and the mingling of tints of rose, pale blue and purplish-pink on the fins, display a combination of colors equalled by no fish outside of the tropics."

The range of the grayling in the United States appears to be limited to Michigan and Montana, while the Arctic species is comparatively abundant in the polar region. In Michigan the fish have diminished at an alarming rate during the past fifteen years, so much so that fears are entertained that it may be exterminated if better measures are not adopted for its protection and propagation—the latter being difficult to accomplish, as the best fish culturists fail in this branch of the work.

In angling for this dainty fish the tackle and methods are almost identical with those used in trout fishing, and the grayling in many instances is found in the same streams with the brook-trout. The American book of the grayling is yet to be published, but when it appears, if prepared by an enthusiastic and practical angler, the work will prove a welcome addition to the library of the fly-fisher.

LAND-LOCKED SALMON, ETC.

"With foam and splash tumultuous
  It dashes on its way,
Past black, basaltic ledges,
  Past boulders, moss'd and gray;
Now dark it sleeps in shadow,
  Mid overhanging woods,
And now reflects the heaven
  In cool transparent floods."

It is now conceded, beyond question, that the land-locked salmon in its structure and natural character is almost identical with the true salmon, from which it differs but little except in size and the habit — natural or acquired — of remaining in fresh water throughout the year instead of making an annual pilgrimage to the sea. Many of the lakes and rivers inhabited by land-locked salmon have direct and easy outlets to the sea, but the fish voluntarily remain, in most instances, near the place of their birth.

In size the fish range from two to seven pounds, though occasionally a heavier one is taken. The list of local names by which it is known would puzzle a novice. In Maine it inhabits the systems of the Sebec, St. Croix, Presumpscot and Union rivers — the latter a tributary of the Penobscot — and the fish is known in that region as the Sebago Salmon, and the Schoodic Salmon; these titles indicating the lake and river most frequented by the land-locked salmon. In the Lake St. John and Upper Saguenay region of the Province of Quebec, the popular name is the Winanishe, Wananishe, or Ouinaniche. Mr. Eugene McCarthy, a practical authority on the subject, accepts and adopts the latter appellation in his book, "The Leaping Ouananiche." The species is also found in the lakes of Labrador, New Brunswick, Ontario and Nova Scotia, in which latter province the fish is strangely enough called the "grayling," although the resemblance is almost wholly imaginary.

Regarding the game qualities of the ouananiche, it is a fish equal to its kindred the sea salmon, so called, due allowance being made for the superior size of the latter. Mr. J. G. Aylwin Creighton, a careful observer, remarks that while watching a fish hooked at the head of Isle Maligne, round which the fiercest rapids of the Grande Decharge sweep, he was profoundly impressed with the remarkable strength and pluck of the ouananiche. Standing thirty feet above the water the angler could see the fish plainly, in the clear stretches between the white-crested rollers, fighting its course up a series of inclines with straight steps of three to four feet at the top of each, and then, after resting a moment on the summit of the fall, dash off like a flash into the full strength of the down-current, from whence the fish was steered into a little cove, and there, fighting until strength was gone, finally lay exhausted on the surface.

Other varieties of the salmon family, differing mainly in size and form, with the same general characteristics, do not require special description here. On the Pacific coast there are several species more or less prized among the anglers of that section.

A western writer classifies the salmon of the Pacific into five species, namely: the quinnat, or tyee salmon; the kisutch, or blue-back salmon; the nerka, or sawqui salmon; the keta, or cultus salmon; the quillayute, or oolahan salmon. The first two species, and the last-named, afford good sport, their respective value as game fish being indicated by the order in which they are named. Trolling and still fishing are the principal methods of capture. The quinnat salmon often attains a weight of one hundred pounds, the blue-back salmon twenty pounds, and the quillayute about six pounds.

Of the smaller species, allied to the common brook trout, there are three that may be referred to as distinct in the region westward of the Rocky Mountains. These species are the California brook trout or rainbow trout; the Rocky Mountain or Yellowstone trout, and the Rio Grande trout. The habitat of each is indicated by its name, and their general character is very similar to the brook trout, the principal difference being in coloration. Many local names are given, as salmon trout, lake trout, bull trout, sea trout, glacier trout, yellowstone trout, geyser trout, cannibal trout, and the like, each having reference to some place or peculiarity distinguishing some one of the three species.

THE CHANNEL BASS.

"But bright, O Florida, the waning year
Smiles o'er thy waters and thy cloud-lands clear;
The fowler comes thy swarming flocks to thin,
The angler comes the luring spoon to spin,
To take by sandy beach or marshy grass
The tarpon, grouper, or the channel bass."

The channel bass is a familiar and highly prized fish in the waters off the southern coast of the United States, where it is known as the red drum by Virginia anglers, the spotted bass by South Carolina fishermen, and the red bass by natives of Georgia and Florida.

By nature the channel bass is bold and omnivorous, the smaller specimens running in schools and following the angler's lure, frequently, to the side of the boat. The fish vary greatly in size, running from one pound to fifty pounds weight. Striped bass tackle is well adapted to channel bass fishing, and the methods are similar.

The Halifax River and Indian River Inlet are favorite resorts, and the months of April and May yield excellent sport on the coast of Florida for lovers of rod and reel. The fish run largest, however, in midsummer, when they are caught in quantities by hand-line fishermen.

THE WEAKFISH.

"But yet a cruel fate prepares
For them its fierce destructive snares;
The fishers with their swarming boats
Spread out their mesh seines and their floats;
The yacht sweeps round them with the sail
Or stoops the sea-hawk in the gale,
While flashing bait and trailing line
Drag them reluctant from the brine."

The weakfish, or squeteague as the Indians call him, is a handsome game fish, symmetrical in outline and rich in colors, its scales shining with the seven cardinal hues. The prevailing tint is blue, and the general appearance of the fish is thus described by ichthyologists: On the back and sides are spots arranged in transverse order. The color of the top of the head is greenish blue; inside of the mouth yellow; gill covers lustrous silver; on lower jaw a salmon tint; fins of different coloration—dorsals brown; pectorals yellowish brown; ventral and anal are orange.

The southern variety of weakfish is known as the salt water trout, and both kinds afford excellent sport for anglers. The summer months, July and August, are best in the North. A fine linen line is used, with a light bamboo rod, a large reel, a good leader, with light swivel sinker, and two hooks of large bend, baited with shedder crab, shrimp, hard clam, or piece of menhaden, to complete the outfit. The weight of the weakfish runs from two pounds to sixteen pounds. Favorite fishing grounds on the Northern coast are at Atlantic City, Newark Bay, Princess Bay, Long Island Sound, mouth of Delaware River, and the Narrows.

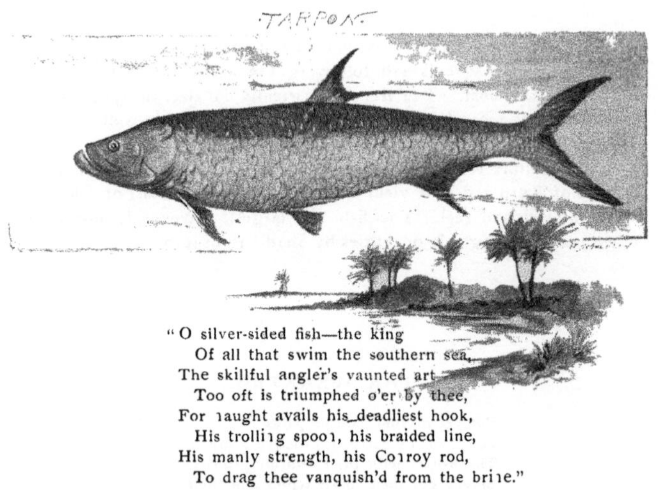

> "O silver-sided fish—the king
> Of all that swim the southern sea,
> The skillful angler's vaunted art
> Too oft is triumphed o'er by thee,
> For naught avails his deadliest hook,
> His trolling spoon, his braided line,
> His manly strength, his Conroy rod,
> To drag thee vanquish'd from the brine."

The silver king—as the tarpon of the Florida coast is often termed—furnishes beyond doubt more exciting sport than any other species of sea fish taken with the rod and reel. As the largest of the herring family the tarpon is often called the king herring, and the prodigious strength, amazing activity, and endless endurance of this armored knight errant among game fishes, combine to make him a most coveted prize in the estimation of adventurous anglers who possess the skill to handle the long line, and the financial ability to carry a long purse well filled.

The late Col. F. S. Pinckney ("Ben Bent"), in his entertaining and practical volume entitled "The Tarpon, or Silver King," supplied a treatise giving elaborate instructions for catching this game fish. Other popular angling writers, notably J. Mortimer Murphy, of Sponge Harbor, Fla., and Dr. Charles J. Kenworthy ("Al Fresco"), of Jacksonville, have contributed valuable articles on tarpon fishing to the sportsmen's journals and standard magazines, so that the pastime is familiar, theoretically at least, to the majority of American anglers.

Along the coast of the United States the habitat of the tarpon is from Texas to the Georgia line—the favorite haunts being in Florida waters, especially St. John's River, Tampa Bay, Tarpon Springs, Punta Rassa, Caloosahatchie, and the Homosassa Rivers. Among the Florida Keys the tarpon may be found at all seasons of the year, and in spring and summer the fish are abundant in many of the rivers and along the coast of Florida.

The tackle for tarpon fishing must be remarkably strong, and during the past ten years (marking the period of time since the species first came into prominence in the category of game fishes)—tarpon rods, reels, lines, etc., have been invented by American manufacturers to meet the rapidly increasing demand. Tarpon fishing in Florida, like salmon fishing in Canada, now attracts a host of distinguished devotees eager for records and recreation. Dr. Kenworthy, describing the sport in his graphic style, says: "We frequently read of the excitement attending the capture of a bronze backer or a speckled trout, but those who give their experiences should hitch on to a tarpon, and they would discover 'music in the air' worth recording; for the capture of a silver king is a bright spot in a fisherman's existence, and a fact worth referring to at a camp fire."

A strong, pliable split bamboo rod, seven to eight feet in length, and of one joint; a Cuttyhunk linen line of fifteen to twenty-one threads in size, and a multiplying reel of the best quality, capable of holding at least six hundred feet of strong line, are of first importance in the way of tackle. To complete the outfit a good supply of strong Limerick or O'Shaughnessy hooks, snoods of piano wire or treble braids of strong cotton line; a serviceable gaff, and other appliances of minor importance will be required.

For bait the mullet is generally taken—sometimes whole, and sometimes only a portion of the fish being used. The bait is allowed to sink to the bottom, in water perhaps eight feet in depth, and the boatman and angler anchored some twenty-five yards away are constantly on the qui vive to begin the battle as soon as the silver king leaps from the water, which he will almost invariably do upon feeling the prick of the hook in his gullet. During the first wild flurry the angler can offer but little resistance, as the series of turns and furious leaps endanger the tackle most at the beginning, but when the 'vaulting ambition' of the tarpon has 'o'erleaped itself,' and the struggle is carried on under instead of above the water, the angler can put his rod and line to the test in order to tire and eventually bring his adversary in reach of the gaff. No finer finny trophy ever graced a table—or adorned a tale—than a well-mounted silver king, gorgeous in his own shining armor, and lying

"Like a warrior taking his rest,"
Bravest and boldest, brightest and best.

BLUE-FISH

"It is a brave, a royal sport,
Trolling for bluefish o'er the seas;
Fair skies and soaring gulls above,
A steady blowing breeze;
A shapely yacht whose foaming prow
The bellowy plain divides,
That like a gallant courser speeds
Far, free o'er ocean tides."

The bluefish has been called the Spanish buccaneer among game fishes of the sea, by reason of its piratical habits, its wanton manner of pursuing its prey—killing smaller fish, principally menhaden or moss-bunkers, in vast numbers, and eating but a small portion of those that are slaughtered. The ocean pirate, variously known as the skipjack, horse mackerel, snapping mackerel, etc., is a valiant game fish, deservedly prized whether on the line or on the banquet board, and all along the Atlantic coast from Florida to Maine the coming of the bluefish is eagerly awaited by anglers and widely heralded by the press each season.

In appearance the bluefish is strong and symmetrical, with graceful curved lines indicating agility and speed. The color is steel blue above and white or greenish white underneath, while the mouth is large and the edges well filled with very sharp teeth, enabling the fish to seize and sever the mossbunkers with great ease. In size the bluefish varies greatly, according to season and locality, the ordinary range being from fourteen to thirty-two inches in length, and from one pound to fifteen pounds in weight, though an instance is recorded of the capture of a specimen weighing twenty-five pounds. This fish was caught in 1874, with rod and reel, at Conasset Narrows, by Mr. L. Hathaway.

It is a singular fact, noted by naturalists, in various works on ichthyology, that the appearance of the bluefish along the Atlantic coast of the United States northward of Carolinas has been irregular. In southern waters the species has perhaps been among the oldest finny inhabitants, but the northern migration, beginning in early spring, has never been regular until within the past sixty years. At present the bluefish ranks next to the striped bass in game qualities, among the sea fishes found in the vicinity of New York and Massachusetts, and in the commercial fisheries, it is exceeded in value only by the codfish and mackerel.

The most popular method of fishing for bluefish is squidding or trolling. This consists in trailing a spoon or squid of ivory, bone or metal, at the end of a line some three hundred feet long, the motive power being a fast sailing sloop or cat-boat, handled by a capable seaman. A heavy sinker should be attached to the line, and some fishermen use a trolley sinker with a large hook set in the end. The schools of bluefish can usually be located by the large number of menhaden jumping from the water in their efforts to escape from the pursuers, and the soaring gulls, frequently hovering close to the surface to pick up the mangled remains of victims killed but not eaten by the ocean pirates, will also point the way for the angler.

A rising tide is considered the best stage of water for bluefishing, but either extreme of the ebb and flood tide may lead on to fishing of good quality. Chumming is a method of fishing also adopted by many sea fishers, the style being similar to that employed in surf-fishing for striped bass. It is said that the bluefish will frequently take the fly—and keep it! If you "have any to bestow, he prefers the large ones, of bright and assorted colors," thus proving his gay and festive nature as a blue blooded buccaneer of the high seas. The bluefish strikes fiercely, and from the instant he is hooked until he is brought to boat the "fun is fast and furious." He fights till the last gasp, sometimes breaking the surface, then rushing deep into the ocean caves, and varying his defensive tactics by darting from side to side, and occasionally coming forward at full speed, overrunning the hooks. Taken all in all (if he is taken at all) the bluefish is a game fish of high rank, and a food fish of excellent quality.

THE STRIPED BASS.

"Where icy currents sweep the banks
Or wash the shores of Labrador,
These finny myriads swarm the seas,
And feed by every shore;
And noblest, bravest of the race,
The striped bass holds foremost place."

Lovers of sea-fishing have very appropriately termed the striped bass "the salmon of the surf." In size, game qualities and as a food fish, the striped bass or rock-fish of the Atlantic coast deservedly ranks with salmo, the leaper. Sea fishermen, enthusiastic over the wild sport enjoyed amid the ocean spray, declare striped bass fishing the grandest and best recreation in the whole realm of angling.

In appearance, this salt water representative of the bass family is symmetrical and handsome. He is described as "cylindrical, tapering; the upper part of the body of a silvery-brown color, the lower part of the sides and abdomen of a beautiful clear silver color; eight or more longitudinal black bands on each side, commencing just back of the opercula, the upper bands running the whole length of the fish, the lower ones terminating just above the anal fin." In size, the striped bass ranges from one pound to one hundred pounds, and an old angler declares that the "delightful uncertainty" in this respect is one of the great charms in this branch of fishing, giving ample scope for all the pleasures of hope and anticipation.

The geographical range of the fish is quite extensive along the Atlantic coast, but the majority of striped bass taken with hook and line, are caught between Cape Cod and Chesapeake Bay. In no other kind of fishing is there such keen rivalry among anglers for the distinction of catching the largest specimen of the season—the honor of "high-line" or "high-hook," as it is usually termed, referring to the greatest fish or the highest number taken. Records are carefully kept by the principal fishing clubs along the Atlantic sea-board, notably, the Cuttyhunk, Squibnocke, Pasque and West Island—showing the weight and number of striped bass caught by the various members from year to year. These records are properly verified, and thus placed outside the category of "fish stories."

Around Manhattan Island, in the East River, Harlem River, the Hudson and New York Bay, are several of the celebrated resorts for striped bass fishing. Hell Gate, a turbulent, foaming channel where the Harlem joins the East River, is probably the most noted locality for the sport in the United States. Several of the prominent angling authorities of America—viz.: "Frank Forester," Genio C. Scott, Hon. Robert B. Roosevelt and Francis Endicott—derived their practical knowledge of bass casting from fishing boats among the swirling eddies of Hell Gate. Large fish were frequently taken there, twenty-five to thirty years ago, but the average catches now are much smaller in numbers and in size, as the fishers have increased ten-fold and the fish have decreased in these waters in almost like ratio.

The term "rock-fish" is often applied to the bass, by reason of the pertinacity with which this game fish clings to rocky channels and reefs, where the waters are churned into spray and foam by changing winds and tide. The smaller bass run together in considerable numbers, and are therefore known as school bass, while the larger specimens are more "sublime and solitary" in their movements.

Of the various methods of bass-fishing, the prime favorite among skilled anglers is surf-fishing, or chumming as it is sometimes called, although the "chumming" is really the work performed by an assistant, in scattering pieces of menhaden broadcast over the waters to be fished. One of the first requisites to success, on the part of the angler, is the ability to make a long and accurate cast in any direction desired. A bona fide cast of two hundred and sixty and one-tenth feet was made by Mr. W. H. Wood, at the tournament of the National Rod and Reel Association, at Central Park Lake; the tackle being such as is commonly used in bass casting, substituting a two and one-half ounce sinker (the average weight of a lobster tail or menhaden bait), in place of the ordinary lure. A cast of less than one hundred feet is seldom successful in surf fishing for striped bass, and long casting will always win, other chances being equal. The angler uses a strong pliant rod, nine or ten feet long, with a large triple multiplying reel holding about four hundred feet of line, best linen make.

The bass fisher usually takes his stand on a small platform, a short distance from shore, enabling him better to reach the haunt of the striped bass at flood tide. Poising his rod, and throwing it back with perhaps three feet of line for play, the angler makes a slow but firm movement forward of the tip, the line spins out rapidly in a graceful curve, and the bait falls easily some two hundred feet away. When hooked, the striped bass is game to the last, and the acrobatic feats he performs, leaping, diving, darting here and there among jagged rocks, struggling for liberty like a runaway race horse with the bits between his teeth, give the excited angler no rest till the fight is won—or lost.

Trolling for bass is another popular style, sometimes with the rod, and occasionally with the line and bait trailed behind the boat. The veteran Louis O. Van Doren says of a peculiar method of fishing witnessed by

himself: "Often we see a solitary boatman leisurely rowing and holding a long and heavy line in his teeth (a sure sign, I take it, that they are his own). How any one's jaws can stand such a strain, I do not know; no doubt though, enthusiasm gives them three-fold strength. I have seen such a lone fisherman rowing along with the stillness and imperturbable gravity of a sphinx, suddenly drop his oars, take the wet line from between his teeth and after a struggle, bring to his basket a three or four-pound striped bass. Imagine what a tooth-pulling strike such a fish must have made."

Fly-fishing, too, may be successfully practiced for a limited season and under favorable conditions of wind and water; but trolling and surf-casting are the methods employed by most anglers in striped bass fishing. Either style should, in the proper season, afford sport exciting enough to satisfy the most ambitious fisher.

Of the localities for striped bass fishing, brief mention has been made. Outside of the immediate vicinity of New York City, some of the noted places are Martha's Vineyard, Block Island, Montauk Point, the Elizabeth Islands (including celebrated Cuttyhunk) and the rocky shores of Massachusetts, Connecticut and New Jersey. Along the coast in the sections indicated, lovers of sea-fishing are in ecstacies when the run of the salmon of the surf is at its height, usually in August and September.

THE MANGROVE SNAPPER.

"Strong be the tackle, for the saw-like teeth
Will cut your silk-worm gut like razor edge,
And firm the hand the mangrove to beguile
From submerged roots, else hook and fish are lost,
For swift it rushes for its secret hole,
And fights and struggles hard while life remains."

This species of fish, a native of southern waters, derives its name from the habit of hiding under the submerged roots of the mangrove, where it lies in wait for its prey, usually the small mullet. It is not a fish of active habits, but is very shy, and the usual method of fishing for this species is to make long casts from the boat, allowing the bait to drop and sink near the holes which it frequents.

The mangrove snapper bears quite a striking resemblance to the small-mouthed black bass, and like its fresh water cousin is an excellent game fish. The ordinary size is from one-half pound to five pounds, but under favorable conditions it grows considerable larger, up to perhaps ten pounds. It feeds freely at night, and in cloudy weather, and furnishes good sport for the angler if he can keep it away from the roots, its natural shelter, for which a rush is made as soon as the hook is felt.

THE BONITO.

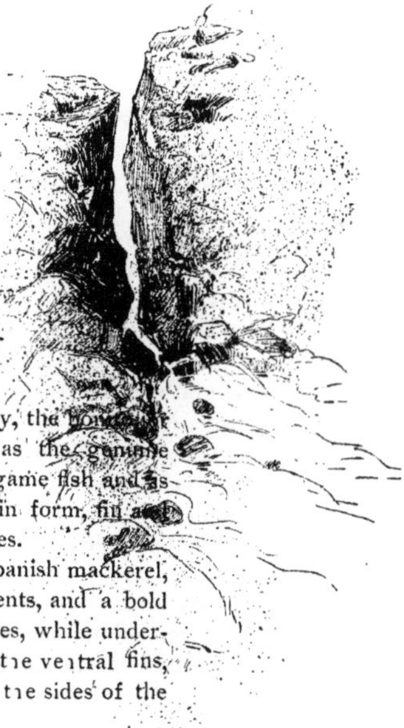

"In all the warmer waters of the world,
The skip-jack swarming shoals are seen,
Where the Sardinian Island rest,
In Mediterranean tides serene,
And where the tumbling billows pour,
Along America's southern shore;
While dense by rocky northern coast
Wanders the countless host."

From his general resemblance to the mackerel family, the bonito, or skip-jack, is often palmed off upon unwary purchasers as the genuine Spanish mackerel, although the latter is far superior as a game fish and as a table delicacy. The bonito is coarser in every respect—in form, fin and flavor, and the angler easily detects the difference in species.

Although heavier in proportion to its size than the Spanish mackerel, the bonito is still a symmetrical fish, swift in its movements, and a bold biter. In color it is of a dark lead tint on the head and sides, while underneath it is an ashen gray. The fins are dark-blue, except the ventral fins, which are white. Six or eight stripes, parallel, run along the sides of the fish.

The bonito usually reaches the northern shores in August and September, at the same time and frequently in company with the bluefish. Anglers often take the bonito while fishing for bluefish, as it will snap at the same bait, and in fact makes almost as desperate resistance when on the line.

Trolling is the principal, almost the only method of angling for the skip-jack, and when time and tide, wind and weather, are favorable, the sport is sufficiently exciting. During the two summer months mentioned, the bonito is quite abundant as far north as Cape Cod, and in no waters of similar latitude is it more plentiful in season than in Massachusetts Bay.

THE BLACKFISH.

"Wherever by extended shore
The rough rocks sow the salty deep,
Wherever kelp and seaweed cling
And crab and starfish crawl and creep,
The blackfish find a lurking place,
Deep in the waters at their base."

Although not highly prized as a game fish by scientific anglers, the blackfish or tautog is an important member of the finny tribe, an excellent food fish, and a ready biter to reward the efforts of juvenile fishers along the wharves.

The blackfish, as indicated by the name, has a black tinge, especially along the back, fading to gray on the sides; the head is large, the back arched, giving the fish a clumsy appearance, but he resists capture in a vigorous manner, and the larger specimens, ten to twelve pounds in weight, are considered prizes even by expert anglers.

As the tautog is one of the earliest of sea fishes to visit Northern waters, arriving in April and remaining until late in October, it is a familiar favorite with the boys and with anglers of larger growth who do not hold tenaciously to the creed that no fish are worth angling for except those that will rise to surface lures. The blackfish feeds along the bottom, in swift, rocky tideways, and narrow channels—the Harlem Kills and little Hell Gate being famous resorts for New Yorkers fond of tautog fishing, though in recent years the species is not found in large numbers near the metropolis.

The best bait for this kind of fishing are sandworms, clams or fiddler crabs; the hook should be of heavy wire, and rest within perhaps a foot of the bottom. With such appliances—similar to the tackle used for weak-fishing—good numbers of blackfish may be taken at Montauk Point, at Barnegat, off Long Branch or Rockaway.

THE KINGFISH.

"Off where the slender light-house lifts,
  Like sheeted ghost, above the surge,
Casting its warning flames at night
  Far to the dim horizon's verge,
Round sunken reef and hidden rock
  Where shells and sands inlay the floor
Of ocean, there the kingfish glide
  And the sea's secret worlds explore."

In Southern waters, where the kingfish is abundant, it is known as the whiting, and in other localities it is termed the barb, but under whatever name it may be designated it is a dainty morsel for the epicure and a gallant fish for the angler. Fifty years ago, when William T. Porter, "Frank Forester," Dr. Bethune, Genio C. Scott, and William C. Prime formed a famous angling coterie in the Atlantic metropolis, the kingfish was found in abundance in the vicinity of New York City. Now it is comparatively scarce in that locality, but in South Bay and off the New Jersey coast it is found in fair numbers during the summer season.

For its size, as compared to other species, the kingfish is one of the gamest inhabitants of the sea. It is long and tapering, and is distinguished for the size of the first dorsal fin, which is high, and adorned

with a long ray. In colors the kingfish is beautiful, varying from a silvery red on the back to bluish white on the abdomen, and the fins are brown, olive and yellow.

In angling for kingfish the tackle is very similar to that used for weakfish, and the favorite baits are sandworms or shedder crabs. Although not a large fish—the range in size being from one to five pounds—the kingfish is gamy in nature, taking the bait boldly, and, when hooked, struggling bravely until brought to boat. The incoming tide is best for the sport, and off the Southern coast the localities for fishing are numerous. In the North the best known points for this branch of angling are Long Branch, Barnegat Inlet, Atlantic City and the south shore of Long Island.

SPANISH MACKEREL.

"Loveliest of all the tribes that swim
The ocean's salty tides,
The Spanish mackerel sweeps the seas,
And like a meteor glides;
It speeds far off the harbor bar,
Where tides are cool and deep,
Shunning the shoals that skirt the shore,
Where the swift bluefish leap."

In delicacy and beauty of color and outline the Spanish mackerel might be found worthy the title of the ocean grayling—lacking that distinctive mark, the banner-like dorsal fin. The fish is very symmetrical in form, and the tail or caudal fin is deeply forked, giving an appearance of swiftness which is in keeping with its movements. It is not often taken by anglers off the coast of the Eastern or New England states, as the fish is found usually in deep waters, farther from shore than the bluefish or striped bass, and is therefore more difficult to locate or pursue. Farther south the fish is more frequently caught, the tackle and style being similar to those used in fishing for bluefish.

Mr. Van Doren, a veteran salt water angler, says of mackerel fishing: "Though sometimes caught by fishermen while bluefishing, yet when a trip is made especially for mackerel it is best to change the bluefish tackle, substituting a smaller spoon and lighter sinker. The Spanish mackerel takes the bait with a snap, makes a short and gallant fight, and when he yields, gives up thoroughly, having no more struggle in him. Off the Southern coast, the capture of Spanish mackerel with hook and line is practiced frequently and with success. The baits used are the same as in bluefishing, and the months when the mackerel appear on the Jersey and New York coast are August and September."

THE SHEEPSHEAD.

"Patient and motionless he waits,
Unmindful of all meaner prize;
His hand upon the humming line,
Fixed on his task his eager eyes;
The flashing bluefish may rush by,
The pig-like porpoise tumble near,
The dusky shark may lash the foam,
And sturgeon from the wave leap clear.
He heeds not—but awaits the jerk
Of sheepshead, down below that lurk."

It is for the hotel perhaps more than for the hook that the sheepshead is prized, but there is considerable skill required and a fair amount of excitement found in fishing for this species. The name is derived from the appearance of the mouth and projecting teeth, giving the fish power to "graze" on the molluscs which adhere to rocks, sunken logs, stakes, etc. This peculiarity is taken advantage of by natives along the Virginia coast who form pens by driving split stakes into the bottom of the sounds or inlets, arranging these stakes in a circle or square, and the molluscs attached thereto form an irresistible attraction for the sheepshead during the annual run or migration of the fish.

The fish is somewhat uncouth in appearance, with its large head, huge projecting teeth and back arched in a great hump, a large dorsal fin running nearly the entire length, armed with strong sharp spines which can be raised or lowered at will. The sheepshead is beautiful in color, however, and is a rare delicacy as an article of food—these qualities relieving the fish of the charge of absolute ugliness.

A stout rod—similar in size to the striped bass rod—a multiplying reel, braided linen line, with swivel and tracing sinker, a double gut leader, a stout hook with short shank, baited with shedder crab or soft clam, will be found a good outfit for still fishing, the usual method of catching sheepshead at Barnegat, Rockaway Beach, Long Branch, Atlantic City, South Bay, and other popular angling resorts. A taut line is necessary to enable the angler to feel the slightest nibble, as the sheepshead is a cautious feeder.

There were knights of shot-gun and rifle,
  Disciples of rod and the reel,
Each telling some tale as a trifle
  To add to the company's weal.
There were stories of camping and shooting,
  All told with abandon and zest,
But the fish tales seem'd to be suiting
  The taste of the brotherhood best.

A jolly party of anglers, eminent in their respective lines of business, and equally famous for skill in casting their fishing lines in pleasant places, had assembled on the banks of the great Nameless River of the North, and were enjoying the glorious sport to be had in the vicinity of Imagination Camp. It was incumbent upon each member to tell "an o'er true tale," or fish story, before breaking camp, and the following collection from the records of the historian of the party, can be taken *cum grano salis*, or with due faith in the everlasting truth of fishing fables in general, and these in particular.

WONDERFUL LEAP OF A SALMON.

One of the old members of the club, Mr. A. W. Courtney, related the following story. Living, as I do, in the city of Buffalo, I have had many opportunities for fishing in Lake Erie, and enjoyed some exciting sport there, but the most thrilling experience of my life in the fishing line was in the rapids below Niagara Falls. Probably few anglers are aware of the fact that in years gone by salmon could be found in comparative abundance all along the Niagara River, up to the falls. Perhaps the salmon have vanished there now, as I understand is the case in the Hudson, where the salmon fishing was good in my boyhood. I was a rather wild and reckless youth, given to daring exploits, and it was an ordinary amusement of mine to fish the Niagara River in a birch bark canoe. My familiarity with the sunken rocks and my skill in avoiding the wildest whirlpools enabled me to escape the fate of Capt. Webb, and other unfortunate adventurers.

On one occasion I hooked a very large salmon, and contrary to the usual custom or habit of the species, he took his course directly up stream toward the falls, and I failed to check him, though I exerted the fullest resistance of the rod and line. As we neared the falls, I felt confident that he would turn, but he still rushed onward until I could feel the spray of the great cataract in my face, and note its power of magnetic attraction drawing my frail craft into the awful vortex of boiling waters.

In my experiments I had contemplated the possibility of such a calamity as this, and was prepared to avoid it. Along the bottom of the canoe was a strong hickory slab, perhaps half an inch in thickness, and running the full length of the boat. In the center I had placed a powerful spiral spring, covered by a circular piece of wood one foot in diameter. Stepping upon this I touched a side lever, and was thrown into the air with amazing force, at a slight angle, as I had previously adjusted the spring with coolness and precision, estimating that it would carry me to the immense rock on the brink of the falls.

The force was barely sufficient to throw me upon the rock, where I found a foothold, and having eased the line which went spinning from the reel with amazing velocity, during my ascent, I was prepared to continue the battle with the salmon. After a short run down the stream the salmon turned, and when some twelve feet distant from the foot of the falls made the most wonderful leap ever recorded, striking the water again just above the crest, and my multiplying reel served its purpose excellently, giving the fish very little, if any, slack line. To make a long story short, I will merely add that the salmon was quite exhausted with his wonderful effort, and was drawn almost unresistingly into my landing net, which I had fastened at my belt and loosened for the occasion, just as the giant game fish turned upon his side and would have floated down the cataract if I had not taken him in just at the right instant.

My adventure was witnessed by but a few people, only one of whom is now living; but I always bless their memory for the aid rendered in rescuing me from my perilous position. If any skeptic doubts the accuracy of my story in a single detail, I can refer him to the life-like picture drawn upon the spot by an artist who witnessed the affair, and through whose kindness the picture will be reproduced in the faithful chronicle of adventures by sea and shore.

A FIGHT WITH A BROOK TROUT.

You have all no doubt heard of the monster trout of the Maine lakes, where they grow to an almost fabulous size, quietly remarked Dr. A. T. Sander, of New York. I had an adventure up there last season, and can vouch for the game qualities of the brook trout in that region. I was fishing in one of the Rangeley lakes, and had caught perhaps fifty trout of large size, but my ambition was, if possible, to break the record. After experimenting with the various flies, which I carried in my fly book, I at last selected a large and gaudy one, nearly equaling a salmon fly in size, and made a cast in a locality where the guide assured me some of the largest trout congregated.

A rise and strike immediately followed. I knew by the vigorous manner in which the trout took the fly that I had a fine gamy fish at the end of the line. Such rushes and wild leaps for liberty you perhaps never saw. All the tactics familiar to experienced anglers were tried in this battle for supremacy, and at the end of half [illegible] hour I was nearly exhausted. I stood in the bow of [illegible] skiff, and the trout in his swift gyrations would [illegible] round and round until I felt dizzy and weak. The[illegible] he would leap from the water, sometimes jumping [illegible] the boat, and apparently trying to entangle the li[illegible] my neck for the purpose of strangling me. Sometimes he would leap back and forth, forming a perfect curve perhaps fifty feet in extent, and his movements were so rapid that I seemed to see a rainbow of colors before my eyes. Once he struck the boat, and the shock nearly threw me overboard.

The guide shared my excitement but managed to keep an outward show of coolness, and his dexte[illegible] the boat prevented it from being overturned. At last, after [illegible]es of fierce struggles the trout was brought within reach of the landing [illegible], and carefully lifted into the boat, where we found by using the [illegible] scales which I had brought with me that the fish weigh[illegible] a full [illegible] pound, and I have always believed that he was even hea[illegible] when making [illegible] fight in the water.

A COAT TAIL AND FISH TALE.

Well, I never had any great luck in fishing, said Mr. George H. Reager, of Philadelphia, but I once had a rather peculiar experience down on the Lycoming in Pennsylvania, with my friend Sylvanus. We spent the whole forenoon fishing, but the sun shone hot, and neither of us had caught a fin. Finally I stopped for lunch, put my basket on the bank, and sat down on a log over the stream, in a shaded nook. I hadn't been there a minute when I felt a jerk at my coat tail, but I knew it was my friend, trying to startle or scare me, so I refused to look around. I just gave my coat a pull and loosened it, and then went on with my lunch.

This happened several times, until finally my patience was exhausted and I jerked my coat tail away spitefully and turned to give Sylvanus a lecture for his nonsense, but bless you, he wan't there. Then I looked up at my basket on the bank, and to my surprise it was full of fine trout. Every time I had jerked my coat tail I flopped a fish into the basket, for I found that the barbless hook, baited with an angleworm, was hanging out through a rent in my pocket with about a foot of line, and I had been doing a good stroke at still fishing without knowing it—"and a very good record for the 'Lie-Coming River,' too," interrupted a listener.

THE REMARKABLE TROUT FRY.

That is somewhat similar to an incident which I recall, said Mr. S. B. Smith, of Dauchy's Agency, one of the quiet men of the party. Three of us, schoolboy chums, were trout fishing in northern New York, and the duties of cook were filled in rotation by each of our trio. On the day referred to, I filled the position of cook, and arose early to prepare breakfast. I partially kindled a camp fire, stuck the keen-pointed, sharp-bladed knife through an overhanging branch, and underneath this placed a board at an angle, and drew a rough outline of a man, with a silver spoon fastened in the crevice representing the mouth.

After this boyish prank, designed to amuse my comrades when they should come out of the tent, I hung the frying pan above the slow fire, and proceeded to the stream, some ten yards away, hoping to catch a few trout for breakfast. I fished by main strength, not by skill, in those days, and although three large trout seized the hook in rapid succession, I lost every one by yanking the rod fiercely and sending the fish spinning through the air, tearing the barb loose.

Becoming discouraged, I was about to return to the tent, when Rob, who had come to the camp-fire, told me to look out for the frying fish or they would be burned to a crisp. Each of the trout I had hooked went in a semicircle, struck the sharp point of the projecting knife, which opened the fish neatly, and in sliding down the board the viscera was removed by the spoon, so that all fell into the frying pan, properly dressed for company, and done brown for the table, when I returned.

AN AIRY FISHING TOUR.

My fishing propensity, said A. L. Thomas, of Lord & Thomas, proved to be the foundation of my fortune. By inclination, almost by instinct in fact, I am opposed to shooting or fishing for the markets, but in the instance referred to, I think you will all agree with me that my course was entirely proper. I was one of the pioneers in the Lake Region of Minnesota, and owned a small farm, but like many frontiersmen my tastes led me to indulge more in the wild sports of the West than in the occupation of a farmer. In one of the lakes, near my farm, the pike grew to large size, and on two occasions I had hooked a monster which broke away, leaving me vexed and more determined than ever to catch him. Finally I decided to put out a long string of set lines running nearly across the lake, and having no special use for a large quantity of fish, I intended to liberate all except the big pike, which I was after.

I rose early the next morning after setting my lines, and found an immense flock of wild geese on the lake. There was a great fluttering and commotion as I drew near, and upon loosening the rope upon which the short lines were attached, the entire flock of geese rose into the air. I had fastened the rope to my wrist, intending to haul in the fish, but to my astonishment many of the hooks had been taken by the geese, and I was carried up into the air trailing after the largest assemblage of fish and fowl I had ever seen. The geese rose to a dizzy height, and then started directly for the North Pole, as nearly as I could estimate.

My position was not a pleasant one, though it was sufficiently exciting. After flying several miles in this manner, the weight of the fish and myself seemed to tire the geese, for they gradually settled down, and finally, much to my relief, the rope became tangled in a huge branch of a hollow tree, which had been broken off at the top. Into this hollow tree I fell to the depth of perhaps ten feet, and discovered that I was standing knee deep

in honeycomb, though fortunately the bees had forsaken the tree. The rope had become loosened from my arm, and I saw no prospect of escaping from my strange prison. Suddenly I heard a prodigious scratching and scrambling outside, and looking up saw a large bear descending backward into the hollow tree. I drew my knife, and as the bear came within reach, grasping him firmly, made a sharp stab which had the effect of starting him out again. As he reached the top, I took a firm hold with one hand and with the other pushed the bear forcibly, overbalancing him so that he fell to the ground, striking on his head, and his neck cracked with a report like a pistol.

I then gathered my scattered senses (together with the geese and fish), and was delighted to find that my home was only a mile distant. By the aid of my horses and wagon I collected the fish and game, shipped them to the best market, and from the proceeds of this shipment and the money received for a ton of first-class honey, I established myself in business. From that day to this I have been able, whenever it was necessary, to catch my fish with a silver hook.

A STRANGE ARTIFICIAL GROWTH.

Not many years ago, said Mr. Frank Alden, of Cincinnati, I owned a private fish preserve, and was fond of making experiments of various kinds in fish culture. A favorite hobby of mine was to observe and record the growth of different species each year. In doing this I fastened a metallic tag to the fish, describing the date, conditions and size of the specimen. As a novelty I once attached a brass whistle to a small black bass, weighing one pound, and one year later caught the same fish, and was surprised to observe a most wonderful phenomenon. Not one of you could guess the remarkable change that had taken place in that length of time. No, the weight of the fish had not increased so greatly as you suppose, in fact, the fish still weighed one pound, but the whistle had increased in size and tone to a large fog horn.

A SOMEWHAT REMARKABLE STORY.

I was passing down Main street, in Rochester, New York, a few days ago, said Mr. Palmer of the H. H. Warner Co., of that city, and my attention was attracted by a large crowd in front of one of the prominent restaurants; edging my way into the crowd, I beheld a large washtub filled with some of the finest specimens of black bass I had ever seen. A placard informed the observer that these black bass had been caught by Mr. John M. Ives, of our company, a day or so before in a creek fifteen feet wide, near Oak Orchard, a country village, about forty miles from Rochester.

Being a lover of game fishing I stepped in to critically examine the fish; after the closest scrutiny I failed to discover a single mark on any of the fish that would indicate they had been caught with a fish hook, and I immediately made up my mind that Mr. Ives or some friend of his had caught the fish in a seine, and I hastened over to the Warner establishment and met Mr. Ives, and our conversation was as follows:

"Hello, John, those are pretty nice fish over there in the window on Main street, and I am puzzled to know how you caught them, for I cannot find a hook mark on them."

"Well the fact is, I was rowing up the stream at night with a lantern brightly burning on the seat before me; I felt something strike the bottom of the boat, and upon investigation found it to be a five-pound bass. Before I could recover from my surprise another bass fell in the same manner, and this strange phenomenon continued quite a while. You see the fish were attracted by the bright light, and they jumped out of the water at it, and fell in the boat."

"This is all right John, but is it not remarkable that the fish did not jump clear over the boat?"

"Not at all. You see I was rowing in the center of the stream and the fish jumped in from both sides at the same time, striking their heads together while over the boat, and fell in an insensible condition. They kept up this strange proceeding until the oil in the lantern gave out, and the light disappeared. I am well satisfied that I could have caught a great many more if the light had lasted longer."

This story may sound rather strange to any person not acquainted with Mr. Ives, but if there be any "doubting Thomases," I would say that Mr. Ives will not only vouch for this story, as being the truth, but he is in a position to prove it beyond a shadow of doubt, as I have seen the lantern myself; and Mr. Ives, if necessary, will make an affidavit that the lantern is now in his possession, this convincing evidence removing every question as to the truthfulness of this story.

THE MUSICAL BASS.

The freaks of nature, both in the vegetable and animal kingdoms, including of course the little fishes in the brook, seem to me really marvelous, said J. L. Stack, the St. Paul Advertising Agent. For instance, at Dellwood lake in Minnesota, which I have owned for many years past, an incident occurred that has entirely changed the habits and characteristics of the black bass inhabiting it. About ten years ago my partner and myself were capsized while sailing, and by a singular coincidence each of us lost a fine gold watch. These watches were exactly alike, and a musical attachment playing the air of "A Life on the Ocean Wave," had been placed in the chromometers by special order. The watches were stem winders, and this particular tune was played each hour in the day.

Of course we both supposed our watches were lost beyond recovery, but last season while fishing in the lake, after an absence of several years from that locality, I caught a monster bass, and you can imagine my astonishment at finding my watch snugly stowed away in the department of the interior. More singular still, it was in perfect order, keeping accurate time, for by some peculiar movement on the part of the fish, the watch had been kept constantly wound up. I found by comparing the time with the watch I carried at the hour of catching the fish that it had not varied two seconds during all the years it had been carried by the bass. The chain, by the way, the bass carried in a sort of negligee fashion, partly hanging through his gill.

But the most wonderful part of the whole affair I discovered later, after catching a few more bass in the same locality. It appears that my partner's watch had also been swallowed by a black bass, and in course of time, through the mysteries of scientific propagation, this musical watch attachment had become hereditary, and every black bass taken in that lake was found to be his own timekeeper, and occasionally the fish danced the Fisher's Hornpipe to their own music in a most amusing manner.

THE ADVERTISING FISH.

Several years ago, when I was living in Texas, I had a somewhat unusual experience, quietly remarked Mr. Wm. C. Hunter, advertising manager of Boyce's Big Weeklies. I am a hunter by nature as well as by name, and spend a considerable time in sport with the gun and rod. On the occasion referred to I was in the Indian Territory, the guest of "a squaw man" at Eufala, and we started on a fishing trip in the Choctaw nation. Arriving at our destination we prepared to worry the festive bass. No sooner did I cast than a large 5¾-pound bass jumped out of the water and took the hook in ten minutes I landed him. I held him up to show my friend, when I noticed a peculiar marking on the belly of the fish, caused by the veins showing through the skin. In a moment my friend caught a bass about the same size and similarly marked. Upon looking at the strange marking we found the veins formed the letters B$\frac{L}{P}$W. We tried in vain to solve the meaning of the veins and started to fish again, and in three hours we caught ninety-three bass, every one marked the same as the first two. I never solved the enigma until about three years ago I told the story to Mr. Boyce, and he smilingly informed me that the letters represented the words: Blade, Ledger, World—Best Paying Weeklies. I saw the connection at a glance.

Mr. Boyce is up to all new schemes for advertising, and I would like to know whether he "fixed" the advertising fish, or whether it was simply a freak of nature, calling the attention of sportsmen to a well-known fact among advertisers.

A LIVELY SPIRIT OF SPIRIT LAKE.

I once had quite a severe fright while fishing by moonlight on Spirit Lake, Iowa. I was usually quite successful in night fishing, and as my business kept me from enjoying the sport during the day time, I nearly always devoted a few hours each evening to angling, said Mr. C. E. Raymond, of Chicago. On the night referred to, a large fish—apparently—seized the hook, and then began the most remarkable struggle I ever experienced. Sometimes the creature was out of the water, sailing along with flapping wings of fins for a distance of fifteen or twenty yards, when it would dive again, all the time making the most vigorous attempts to

There were knights of shot gun and rifle
Disciples of rod and the reel,

Each telling some tale as a trifle
To add to the company's weal.

escape, my line meanwhile humming a very lively reel. When in the air it would utter a weird and mournful sound that could be heard for miles.

I am not naturally superstitious, but this caused nervous chills to creep over me, as the legends of Spirit Lake were of such a character that I imagined I might have caught the ghost of some departed lake monster. Finally, after about fifteen minutes, the creature was secured, and I discovered it to be a large loon, while the attendant excitement nearly made me a lunatic.

FUN WITH FLYING FISH.

Mr. Lyman D. Morse, of the Bates & Morse Agency, considered the the most unassuming member of the club, told the following modest tale: For the benefit of my health I took an ocean voyage, a few years ago, and to fully enjoy my trip I carried a complete outfit for fishing and shooting. Our ship was a sailing vessel, and we lay becalmed for a week on the line of the equator, with the midsummer sun fairly boiling the surface of the ocean, so that it seemed like an immense seething cauldron. This condition of affairs was very monotonous to everyone except the cook, who made the best of it by doing a little deep-sea fishing every day, and cooking his fish in the ocean brine as he held them at the top of the water for a moment.

The flying fish were too sharp to be caught by still fishing, and too swift to be lingering around near the boiling point, which was only about a foot in depth. Large schools of these fish could be seen in various directions, darting up through the hot surface water, and cooling their fins and bodies by a long flight in the shadow of our sails. The fish became quite sociable, and evidently had a larger degree of intelligence than most members of the finny tribe.

To while away the time it occurred to me that we might have some amusement by attaching small flags to the fish which we caught, and in a short time we produced a combination which gave a surprising effect by starting a dozen different fish from the boat at one time, with the emblems of twelve different nations. The fish evidently enjoyed the sport, and would return voluntarily to be placed in line and take a new flight, with waving banners in the air.

AN EYE FOR AN EYE.

Mr. J. B. Rose, of Chicago, known as the modest man of the club, told the following story: In my youth I was a more persistent and enthusiastic angler than at the present time, and I shall always keep vividly in mind the exciting incident I am about to relate. After completing my college course I devoted three months' time to out-door sports, principally fishing, and during my rambles with the rod, located a very large fish in a deep pool, below the rapids of White River, so called on account of the breakers and foam along the frequent cascades.

I had observed, on more than one occasion, the huge form of this fish, always in the same pool, breaking the surface as he feasted on the natural flies, or leaping in play when the rising or setting sun tinged the waters, but he seemed insensible to the attraction of my best lures, and most taking ways. My summer outing was nearly over, and I determined on a final effort to catch the king of the pool. As I approached the spot I observed that he was taking his morning meal in dignified leisure, but to my consternation a colored gentleman of African descent was just preparing to cast his primitive hook and line, he being partially shielded from view by the overhanging boughs and a huge boulder which intervened between us.

The colored angler evidently had the right of way in the fishing line, and I decided to watch developments. His bait was a live minnow, and he prepared with due deliberation to make his cast where the large fish had been rising. His first cast was unsuccessful, and he retrieved the line by jerking the pole backward, evidently intending to throw his bait a little further up the stream at the next attempt. His whole mind and energy seemed bent on the capture of the fish, and subsequent developments proved the mastery of mind over matter. By some means the pole struck an overhanging branch in its backward cast, and the line was diverted from the course intended. The minnow was jerked from the hook, which flew backward and struck the angler fairly in the eye. The pain must have been excruciating, but so intent

was he upon the work before him that the forward cast was made exactly in accordance with his original intention, the eye was jerked from its socket and fell in the water at the spot which he had intended to reach with the minnow. The fish seized it eagerly, and then began a most remarkable battle which ended, by my assistance, in the capture of the fish.

During my college course I had made a special study of the human eye, with the intention of becoming an oculist, and the knowledge thus gained proved of great value to me in this emergency. Fortunately my case of instruments had been placed in my coat pocket, and observing that the eye of the fish was almost identical in size and color with that of the angler, I determined to make a remarkable experiment in surgery. Carefully removing the eye from the fish, I placed it in the socket from which the negro's lacerated optic had been torn, and connected the severed nerve so deftly that within a few minutes, the negro was able to take a glance at the fish with the borrowed eye taken from the fish captured. At the present time scarcely any difference can be detected in the eyes of the colored angler, except that the one transplanted from the fish has a slight "cast" in it.

BUFFALO SHOOTING ON THE WING.

Perhaps you never heard of shooting buffalo on the wing, said Mr. Conrad Budke, of St. Louis. I do not, of course, mean the wild buffalo recently described in the *Saturday Blade*, referring to a long-lost herd discovered somewhere out West. The kind I have reference to is the buffalo fish, to be found in the Southwest. It is one of the gamest fish in Louisiana. The bayous overflow all the flat country, which at certain seasons is covered to a depth of about twelve inches, affording excellent feeding grounds for the buffalo fish.

The local sportsmen and planters manage to have excellent sport in this way: On finding a herd—I mean a school—of buffalo fish, the chase begins. Upon reaching the board fences, which run across the overflowed fields, the fish take flying leaps, and gunners stationed along the line pick them off by snap shots. Some of the expert shooters use repeating rifles, and it is very exciting sport, especially when the buffalo, arising from the water on all sides, fly over the fences, the boats, submerged brush leaps, and even the dwarf trees growing along the lowlands.

A GOOD ELECTRIC EEL.

Dr. R. V. Pierce, of Buffalo, gave the following interesting story: I do not, as a rule, reveal any of my business secrets, but as we are all brother anglers, and as my success in life is so closely identified with fish and fishing, I will relate a little story, 'not necessarily for publication, but as a guarantee of good faith,'—to use the newspaper phrase. Many years ago, before I became a practicing physician and specialist, I was fishing in a certain locality which it is not necessary to name, as I might by so doing give some shrewd practitioner a chance to establish himself as a competitor in the same line of business with myself.

After making a moderate catch I was about to give up fishing for the day, when a strange fish took my bait, and upon attempting to remove it from the hook I received a shock which convinced me that I had captured an electric eel, or more correctly, perhaps, an electric eel had captured me. The violence of the electric shock nearly prostrated me, but I recovered sufficiently to remove the eel from the hook, using a pair of gloves in doing so. The fish seemed to be very intelligent, and I placed it in a pail of water, and carefully took the specimen home alive.

While a medical student I always had great faith in electricity, where properly administered, and here was an opportunity to make use of the magnetic current from a natural source. My first study was to completely domesticate and educate the electric eel. Within a short time the eel, which I kept in a small tank, would come to me in response to a beckoning call, and by degrees I learned him to control the electrical power which he would communicate to me, or through the medium of a wire, in proportion to the amount of pressure brought to bear upon him. I now began advertising my electrical cure for various diseases, and with the eel concealed, yet under perfect control, I performed some almost marvelous cures, establishing my reputation throughout the United States. The power of the fish in this direction developed wonderfully with practice, and by the aid of a few assistants and a simple system, I have treated no less than one hundred patients at one time, the sole source of electricity being my electric eel.

At one time when the electric light plant of our city failed temporarily, I offered my assistance, and for two nights supplied a brilliant light to all portions of the city, but this proved to be a severe strain upon my eel, and I would not repeat the experiment for love or money, as I value the health of my medical assistant too highly.

Many of my brother anglers have marveled at my success in fishing, but the secret, which I have never before revealed, is simple. Within the butt of my fishing rod is a commodious cavity, extending nearly the whole length, giving room for my electric eel, where he rests comfortably, covered with a thin layer of moss, which I keep constantly moistened. Instead of an ordinary silk or linen line, I use a minute and almost invisible wire. This is conducted through the rings into the butt of the rod, and a small electrical bell tinkles within whenever a fish strikes the hook. My electric eel immediately seizes the end of the wire, and the electric shock invariably causes the fish to make a convulsive leap out of the water, after which, by regulating the current, I can have several minutes exciting sport, if desired ; or where the fish is an extremely large one, a concentrated shock will deprive him of power at once, and make him an easy victim. I use the same tackle whether fishing for black bass, salmon, or tarpon, and my friends have been astounded to find such large fish could be caught upon such a delicate line and light rod.

On one occasion I caught a shark weighing perhaps a thousand pounds with less effort than it would require for an ordinary angler to land a two-pound trout. I would not hesitate, if I were a betting man, to wager one thousand dollars that I could land a whale easily with my electrical fishing apparatus, though of late I am very careful to avoid testing the full powers of my faithful accomplice in the angling art.

THE SYMPATHETIC SAWFISH.

The shark has an evil reputation in all parts of the world, remarked Mr. C. F. David, the Boston "attorney at advertising," but I have a very grateful recollection of a service done me by the sawfish, which is a sort of cousin of the shark family. While prospecting for pearls and coral, many years ago, I was suddenly caught by a large devilfish, and would have been killed undoubtedly if I had not been liberated by the sawfish. This fish seeing my critical situation, immediately attacked the devilfish, sawing off every arm of the sea monster, and allowing me to reach the surface, nearly dead. In fact I was so severely injured that I could not swim, and the sawfish rose underneath me and carried me ashore on his back in a very gentle manner. I have never been fully convinced whether this action was mainly out of sympathy for me, or to spite the devilfish, which is, no doubt, a natural enemy of the sawfish.

AN ENCOUNTER WITH A SHARK.

That puts me in mind of an adventure I had some years ago off the Florida coast, remarked Wm. Hill, the watch man at Chicago, who "pays the express." My principal object in visiting Florida was to enjoy the tarpon fishing, but incidentally I found much excitement in another direction. Sharks were exceedingly plentiful, and I finally concluded to vary the recreation of tarpon fishing with a cruise after these cruel sea pirates. Provided with strong tackle and a capable boatman, I anchored my skiff near the inlet where quite a number of sharks could be seen daily, frisking about in the surf, ready to battle with man or fish. My previous experience had especially fitted me for an encounter of this kind. During fifteen years of my life I had been an active speculator, and was thus brought into daily contact with the worst variety of land sharks, and I knew the sea sharks could not equal them in craft or cruelty. In my experience with land sharks it was not an uncommon thing to see one of them swallow a whole railway line and a million acre land grant without change of countenance.

But to return to my story. After catching a few comparatively small specimens I was beginning to long for something more exciting, when suddenly a monster shark was seen a short distance away, apparently in just the mood for war. He swallowed the bait, and the strong line went spinning into the depths with a rapidity which could not be checked. This could not last long. The line had nearly run off the windlass, which served the purpose of a reel, at the end of the boat. It finally broke off short, capsizing the boat and throwing myself and assistant into the water. I at once seized the vanishing end of the rope, and, strange as it may appear, swam to the shore, drawing the shark after me and landed him safely on the beach, where, upon measurement, he was found to be twenty feet in length. Since that time I have never been afraid to cope, single-handed, with the largest of the species to be found in the ocean, but have found the land sharks more difficult and dangerous to handle.

A RARE CATCH.

"Well," remarked Mr. Draper, of Geo. P. Rowell's Agency, "Mr. Fred Ringer, of our agency, and I took a day off last season and went down to Geneva lake for a quiet fish. We obtained a boat and rowed out to the middle of the lake and made ready for business. Putting on a live frog Mr. Ringer made one of his famous long distance casts. A gull see-

ing the flying bait made a swoop for it and sailed away. Mr. Ringer saw five hundred feet of mist-colored silk line reeled away into the heavens in a most amazing manner in the wake of a pair of broad white wings that flashed in the sun.

"What on earth have you caught?" I cried to my friend.

"Blamed if I know," was the quiet reply, as the whizzing reel spun round, "but I think I have got a cherubim!"

A RAILWAY FISHING LINE.

Perhaps you never heard how our railway obtained the name of the fishing line, said Mr. F. H. Miller, of the C. M. & St. P. R. R., Chicago. It happened in this way: "One of the officers of the road, accompanied by a friend, went up to a favorite lake on a fishing trip several years ago. They were fishing for black bass and mascalonge. Each one caught a large number of black bass, and several mascalonge of fair size, but this did not satisfy them. They wished to bring home one of the large specimens known to inhabit the lake, as a well-mounted mascalonge in a street window is the best kind of advertising for any railway line desiring the patronage of anglers. I should have explained that our line, at the point referred to, runs along near the border of the lake for some distance, and then turns at an angle into the wilderness.

One morning Mr. B—— and his friend started out on a hand car from a little way station, intending to take a fishing boat upon arriving at the lake to enjoy a few hours sport among the mascalonge. Just for amusement Mr. B—— threw out the trolling spoon and perhaps twenty yards of line, as the hand car drew close to the lake. The artificial bait began spinning swiftly through the water, and in less time than it takes to tell it, a huge mascalonge had seized the lure. The fish turned in its course, after running out in the lake a short distance, and swam along parallel with the shore at marvelous speed. By some means the line became tangled in the handle bar of the hand car, and the mascalonge led the anglers a race along that half-mile course that would put to shame the best efforts of an American Derby winner at Washington Park. The water frothed and foamed in the wake of the fish, and the hand car dashed along the rails like a lightning express train.

When the point was reached where the railway line diverged from the lake shore, it was expected that the line would break, but its strength proved equal to the emergency. The hand car was running at the rate of a mile a minute, and the fish was drawn ashore before it had time to use its great power of resistance. The mascalonge was, of course, not familiar with this overland trail and in floundering through the underbrush and among the trees the scales flew in a shower in every direction. When the hand car was stopped a half mile further on, nothing remained of the fish except his head, which was preserved in good condition. To give some idea of the struggles made by the fish during the short journey through the wilderness, it is only necessary to state that the ends of the ties were torn off for quite a distance, and many small saplings, enough to make a carload of rustic fish poles, were torn up along the way. This little adventure fairly entitles our railway to the name of 'the fishing line.'"

A NEW FISHING REEL.

Speaking of popular fishing resorts, remarked Mr. T. G. Wiles, of Kansas City, Mr. C. M. Lucas, my partner in the Advertising Agency business, and I once conducted a hotel for anglers and sportsmen in northern Missouri. Game was abundant in that vicinity, and several species of game fish could be found in the lake and river near the hotel. The experienced anglers visiting that region always secured large catches of fish, but frequently some ambitious men from the cities, having no knowledge of fish and fishing, would be disappointed, as their efforts in the way of angling reminded one of the old time style of flailing on a threshing floor. This of course frightened away the black bass and other game fish, so we were obliged to invent something which would secure a well-filled creel for each one, as we could not afford to lose their patronage.

We were quite expert in fly fishing, and we quietly manufactured something in the form of a windmill, and attached to each arm of this unique fishing machine a good length of fine line, and by way of bait would place a neat artificial fly at the end of one line, a grasshopper upon the next, and other attractive lures upon the remaining lines. With a good breeze the fishing apparatus would work automatically, and everything was so adjusted that the baits would fall upon the water as light as a thistle down. When there was no breeze, an assistant was employed to run this fishing reel, and some of the largest catches of game fish in that region were, in this way, made by men who knew nothing about practical angling.

For those who preferred still fishing, we had another system, which worked equally as well. A dozen tame ducks, each having a line attached to one leg, would be placed in the water at some suitable point, and when a fish seized the hook the duck would swim directly for the boat. Sometimes the struggle would be a severe one, but with the aid of the boatman the duck could always be depended upon to win. Unfortunately, we never obtained a patent on either process, and I expect it has been adopted by many other hotel proprietors throughout the country.

FISHING ON A FOG BANK.

Mr. Frank B. Stevens, of Boston, referring to a peculiar incident in his fishing career, said: My favorite branch of angling has been that of sea fishing along the Massachusetts coast. Striped bass fishing and blue fishing furnish excellent recreation for me. The heavy fogs have at times interfered, to some extent, with my sport, especially when out a short distance at sea in a light skiff or sailing boat. However, I survived the dangers of the sea, and in reality the greatest peril I ever encountered was when surf fishing for striped bass and casting from the shore, my position being upon a high ledge of rocks. The fog, which was almost impenetrable, had crept down gradually until I could scarcely see the curling waves which dashed in against the rocks below my feet.

I was perfectly familiar with the locality and continued the sport, but as the fog grew more dense I shifted my position, drawing close to the edge of the rocks, the ledge seeming to extend farther into the surf at this point than I had formerly supposed. Working my way gradually forward and keeping close to the extreme edge, I finally secured a strike, and was playing my fish scientifically, when the sun shining through a rift in the clouds began to dispel the dense fog. As the fog began to disappear over the bay and roll inland, I was astonished and alarmed to find that in my eagerness to keep close to the edge of the rocks overlooking the surf, I had gone entirely beyond the rocky cliff and was standing upon the edge of the fog bank nearly a hundred yards from shore. The waves were rolling heavily over the rocks below, and it was only by the greatest exertion that I scrambled back, managing to keep pace with the receding fog bank until I reached the rocks again. I lost my fish, of course, but was glad to escape with my life.

AN O'ER TRUE TALE.

There is something truly marvelous in the 'moving adventures by flood and field,' which form a part of the experience of every angler and sportsman, said Mr. Willard Everett, of Hood's Sarsaparilla fame. The public seems to be skeptical, and these adventures, especially in angling, are looked upon as fish stories. I will mention a little incident which once occurred to me, when I was fishing up in Vermont, where game and fish are very plentiful. I was floating for deer, and shot at a large buck, which stood in the edge of the lake, when a monster trout sprang into the air between myself and the deer, and the bullet passed through both. The bullet went whizzing on, and as I was curious to find where it finally struck, I drew the boat ashore and discovered that the ball had entered a bee tree, from which a stream of pure honey was flowing. Closing the bullet hole with one finger, I reached around with the other hand to find something to stop the flow of honey. A cub bear, attracted by the scent of the honey, was just approaching, and seized my hand, biting it quite savagely. In my excitement I caught hold of the cub and threw it backward several yards, breaking its neck and at the same time killing three partridges. On returning to the boat and looking for the deer, I found that the buck upon being shot had made one plunge forward into deeper water, and in doing this had struck five large trout, which were impaled upon the points of his antlers. Although I had started out for a hunting trip, it resulted in making quite a successful fishing tour.

A FIGHT BETWEEN BULLHEADS.

Most varieties of fish seem to be born fighters, with the nature of cannibals, remarked Mr. Marcus Wight, of J. C. Ayer & Co., Lowell, Mass. The most furious fight I ever observed between fish was on the upper Mississippi. It was by two bullheads of large size. The water was quite clear, and I could observe every movement plainly. Before each attack the bullheads would rise to the surface and utter a peculiar bellow, and then rush at each other with a savage fury, shaking their horns in a manner similar to that of their bovine kindred on land. To me it mattered little which of the bullheads won the battle, but I could not help a feeling of sympathy for the vanquished fish, after seeing him thrust and gored almost to death by the victor. The water was stained with blood for some distance around, and the sound of the conflict could be heard over the waters for many miles.

FISHHAWK VS. FLYING FISH.

The fishhawk is a most inveterate enemy of all the smaller species of fish, and it is seldom that any inhabitant of the water can hope to battle with this bird with any expectation of success, said Mr. Pettingill, the Boston Advertising Agent. However, I once noticed a strife between a flying fish and fishhawk, which resulted in a victory for the former. The fishhawk had pounced down on the flyingfish, which escaped the talons of the bird, and then began the struggle for life. Of course the flyingfish might have avoided the battle by remaining deep in the water, but the unprovoked attack had evidently aroused its anger. The hawk hovered close over the water, and the fish, with remarkable agility, would fly at it from beneath, and finally it struck the bird in the middle of the body, passing entirely through, and killing the fishhawk on the spot. It was quite an exciting affair, and my sympathies were with the flyingfish from the first.

NO USE FOR THIS COUNTRY.

The salmon in the streams in Washington and Vancouver will not rise to a fly like their sportier cousins in Maine, said Dr. A. H. Hayes, of Boston. When the boundaries between the United States and the British possessions were being surveyed, Great Britain sent a Sir W—— as her representative to look over the territory, and to make a report to her Majesty the Queen. Sir W—— was an ardent sportsman, and seeing so many salmon in the streams, he started after them with a fly, but the fish came not up for the fly, neither did they bite any other artificial bait, and Sir W——'s opinion of the country was expressed in his official report to the Queen, as follows: "The blooming country is not worth a d——n, the salmon there will not rise to a fly."

BARTERING WITH A JEWFISH.

Mr. J. Walter Thompson, of New York, told an incident to illustrate the fact, that fish, like men, have their strong personal traits. He said: "Down in the South the jewfish is not considered worthy of special note or attention as a game fish, but on account of his size he sometimes furnishes much excitement for fishermen. The jewfish occasionally attains a weight of over five hundred pounds, and as it has great strength, will frequently break a hook large enough to capture a shark. The jewfish has sometimes been called a giant perch, but I should prefer to translate his name literally, and call him an aquatic Hebrew, on account of an occurrence which gave evidence, to my mind, of the ability of the fish as a financier.

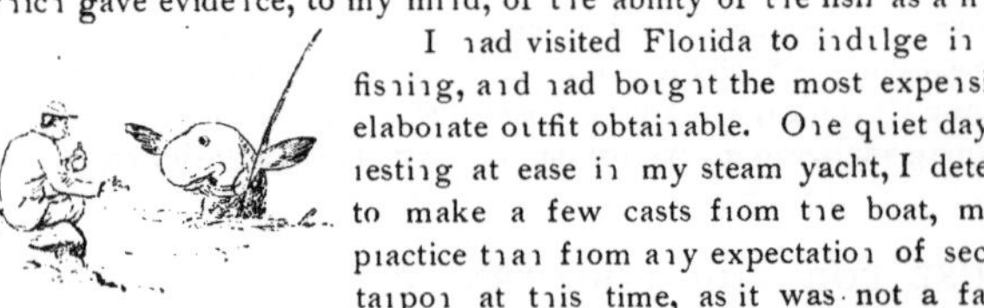

I had visited Florida to indulge in tarpon fishing, and had bought the most expensive and elaborate outfit obtainable. One quiet day, while resting at ease in my steam yacht, I determined to make a few casts from the boat, more for practice than from any expectation of securing a tarpon at this time, as it was not a favorable locality for fishing. On making the second cast a monster jewfish took the bait, and would have taken the line, rod, reel and all thereunto belonging, if I had not succeeded in making a compromise. I knew that I could not fight successfully against the giant strength of the jewfish, and by a series of peculiar movements with his pectoral fins the fish conveyed to me, in language almost as intelligible as words to one familiar with the gestures of clothing dealers on Chatham street, that he would deliver the goods for a proper consideration.

I was not in a mood to barter with the aquatic Hebrew, but under the necessity of the moment concluded it advisable to make a deal. Knowing the intense love of gold on the part of both the land and water species, I asked my assistant to hold up to the jewfish a glass aquarium filled with handsome goldfish. I held up my left hand with three fingers extended, to indicate that I would give three goldfish to recover my line and tackle. The jewfish shrugged his shoulders and shook his head savagely by way of refusal, and I immediately raised my bid to five, which was also refused. I was finally obliged to give that jewfish the whole job lot of goldfish to obtain my tackle again, although I always considered it an unfair advantage unworthy of any except a salt-water Shylock, and I have never associated with jewfish from that day to this.

A LIVE ARTIFICIAL FLY.

Mr. Wm. Boyle, the "Golden Specific" man, of Cincinnati, referring to scientific fly casting, mentioned the following incident in his career: I was fishing in a rocky stream, where remarkable skill is required to secure a full creel, as the trout were educated, so to speak, to avoid the ordinary wiles of the angler. On the occasion alluded to, I threw a fly so far and so delicately that, as it hovered close to the water, it took life and was about to make use of its wings to soar away, when a huge trout, seeing it rise from the surface, made a leap and turned the course of the insect's travel from the upper air to the bottom of his throat. It is generally known that natural flies originate from dead matter, and I had always believed it possible for any man of inventive genius to transform a handsome artificial fly into a live one, so my experiment simply proved the theory.

ONE SWALLOW TOO MANY.

Speaking of live bait, said Mr. Chalmers, of the National Manufacturing & Importing Co., Chicago, I had an amusing experience a few years ago in the lake region of Wisconsin. I was fishing for black bass, with a bait rod, and having good sport, when suddenly the minnow fell from the hook just as I was making a cast. As the minnow fell a swallow darting by was caught on the hook, and dropped struggling to the water, where it was seized by a large bass. I proceeded to reel in the fish, but an instant later a huge mascalonge swallowed the bass, and the reel sang a livelier tune than ever before. I felt doubtful about my ability to land the mascalonge, but by careful work I exhausted the fish, and in about twenty minutes had the satisfaction of bringing it to the gaff and secured it in good style. As a singular fact I observed that upon taking the bass from the throat of the mascalonge and loosening the hook, the swallow was found to be alive, and flew away as soon as it was liberated. I always regarded it as an excellent illustration of the evil of taking one swallow too many—a moral which amused the listeners at the expense of the narrator.

THE PETRIFIED ANGLER.

While attending the World's Fair last summer, I observed with much interest the lifelike figure of the Ideal Still Fisher, as represented in the Government Building, said Mr. H. B. Humphrey, of Boston. It reminded me very forcibly of the petrified fisherman, a negro, who has been sitting from time immemorial on a rock beside the Emory River. The pose, a half sleepy, half expectant attitude, is perfect, and one might imagine this solid Muldoon to be a living angler in a somewhat rocky condition. The story in brief was published some time ago in the *Saturday Blade*, I believe, and I understand from the reporter of that enterprising paper that he would have vouched for the accuracy of the tale in every particular, but for the fact that the petrified fisherman refused to be interviewed, and would not give an affidavit as to his identity. Such care is very commendable, but rare in modern journalism.

A PERSISTENT BITER.

The homing instinct of catfish seems to be equal to that of domestic cats, remarked Mr. J. R. Griffitts, advertising manager of the C. B. & Q. R. R. To illustrate this, I will relate a little anecdote. I was fishing in a bend of the Mississippi River for pickerel, knowing that several large ones inhabited that particular pool. By some peculiar fatality every time I cast my line a large catfish took the hook, and as I did not care for this species of fish I liberated it each time and placed it farther down the stream, trusting that it would not trouble me again. Finally I became angry at the persistency of the catfish, and cut off his head, throwing both the head and body back into the river.

You know the mouth of the catfish is immense in the fullest sense of the word, but I was surprised when I made my next cast to find that this fish had swallowed his own body, which passed through the decapitated head and by a sort of natural attachment was fastened to it again, and the fish took my bait as eagerly as before. Seeing that the fish was determined to eat himself out of house and home, and become an outcast, I cast him out on the bank and let him graze on the shrubbery until I completed my fishing.

A FISHY REVIEW.

Did you ever notice, said Mr. George G. Parvin, of Cincinnati, the methodical habits of the various species of fish. It is, no doubt, on account of their systematic habits and custom that fish usually go in schools, where they receive their education, fitting them for their respective walks or swims in life. I once noticed down at the inlet of Indian River, in Florida, where the tide-water from the ocean mingles with the fresh waters of the stream, a wonderful congregation of fishes of all varieties. They were leaping about in play, and over the waves I could hear the sounds of the fish language in all their dialects.

There was the muffled drumming of the drumfish, the bellowing of the buffalofish, the satisfied grunting of the hogfish, the neighing of the redhorse, the barking of the dogfish, the caterwauling of the catfish, and the bleating of the sheepshead, mingled with other sounds too numerous to mention.

I observed, too, the characteristic movements of each species: the floundering of the flounders, the soldier-like pace of the sergeant fish, the dainty walk of the ladyfish, and the peculiar grouping of the groupers; but what interested me most was the grand review which took place just before the fish party broke up. The swordfish brandished his sword and led the way, while the sawfish saw that the drill was properly conducted. The kingfish, upon a coral reef, reviewed the procession. The National colors were borne by the red grouper, the whitefish and the bluefish, and the music was furnished by the black drum.

The weakfish was assisted by the rockfish, and in regular order followed the shad, in his shadow, the pickerel with a pick, the pike-perch with his pike, the skip-jack skipping along, the carping sea-carp, the rock bass looking rocky, the straw bass carrying straw, the calico bass in a calico garb, the sunfish with its attendant shiners, the star fishes; the moon-eye, looking moon-struck; the lake lawyers and their twin pettifoggers, the bill fish, presenting their bills; the shovel-nose sturgeon, shoveling his way; the horned club shaking his horns, and many other kinds of fish, each in its proper place, in the unique procession. It seemed like a sort of watery congress of all nations—a marine Midway Plaisance, with all the finny features imaginable. A greater variety of scaly customers I never saw.

BROADSWORD FIGHT WITH A SWORDFISH.

My skill with the sword once saved my life, said Mr. L. S. Allen, of the B. & O. R. R. It happened in this way. Soon after graduating with honors at West Point, I was taking a cruise at sea, and frequently whiled away my time by practicing the broadsword exercise with one of the officers on the vessel, who was quite an expert in the art. We were practicing one day, when by an unlucky stumble, I fell overboard, still retaining the sword in my hand. Upon rising to the surface the first thing that met my gaze was a swordfish not ten feet away, making directly at me. My presence of mind did not desert me, for although I was entirely out of my element and the swordfish had the advantage in this respect, I realized that coolness might save my life.

The fight was, beyond doubt, the most peculiar one ever fought with swords. My adversary was no novice in the science, and the vigor of his direct thrusts was something terrific. I escaped injury as much by my agility as by my skill in warding off his attacks. After receiving a flesh wound and in return gouging out an eye of my antagonist, the battle became fast and furious. At last I succeeded in blinding the remaining eye of my enemy, and then I had him at my mercy. With one fierce stroke I disarmed him, or in other words severed the sword from his vicious looking head, and catching it as it was sinking, threw it on board the ship.

My victory seemed to give me new strength and courage. Seizing the now defenseless swordfish by one of his fins I swam easily to the side of the ship, and when a rope was lowered drew him up with me to the deck. I still possess his sword as a relic, and at the time was warmly congratulated for my combined skill and strength. The swordfish was weighed soon after I carried him on deck and was found to tip the beam at two thousand pounds.

A PATRIOTIC SPECIES OF GRAYLING.

Over in Michigan, said Mr. Charles H. Fuller, the Chicago Advertising Agent, the principal game fish, or at least the most beautiful, is the grayling. You know the scientific name of this fish is *Thymallus Tricolor*, the latter having reference to the three beautiful colors with which it is adorned. For many years past I have taken great pleasure in grayling fishing, and it occurred to me that by systematic breeding the coloration of the fish could be controlled and modified, to a certain extent, thus making a distinct branch of the species, peculiarly American.

With this idea in my mind, I began a systematic and elaborate system of fish culture, selecting the best specimens, and by a method originating in my own brain, I finally succeeded in producing a beautiful combination of colors. The dorsal fin of the grayling is its chief mark of beauty, rising to a height of perhaps three inches, extending along the back nearly half the length of the fish, and waving in the clear water like a beautiful banner, with rainbow tints. In the arrangement of colors I have secured a blending in regular order of the red, white and blue, and at the lower half of the fin, close to the back, my new species shows the stars in perfect arrangement, after the style of the American flag.

Having accomplished this, I determined to train the fish and put them to practical use. Through careful breeding I have succeeded in obtaining quite a number of grayling in which the pectoral fins and the caudal fin, or tail, were abnormally developed. By proper encouragement the fish soon learned to take prodigious leaps from the water, and finally developed into a distinct variety of flying fish. They are also sensible to the charms of music, and now it is my custom on the Fourth of July, on Inaugural Day, and every other patriotic occasion, to call the fish from the water, by the aid of a band playing the inspiring air of the "Star Spangled Banner," to which tune my educated grayling keep perfect time, and fly over the lawn in battalions to the admiration of all observers.

A TOOTH FOR A TOOTH.

That reminds me, said Mr. W. B. Duffy, the Malt Whisky man, of an adventure I had once upon a time off the shores of Staten Island. This was my favorite resort for striped bass fishing, and many a big one have I caught there in former days. One afternoon I had exceptionally good luck, catching several bass of fair size, and after sunset, as I stood on a projecting rock watching the rise and fall of the water, and listening to what the wild waves were saying, a strange melody was borne to my ears. It was soft and plaintive, with a peculiar tone like that of an æolian harp, and one could almost imagine mingled with it a subdued siren song, which seemed to come out of the depths of the ocean. The words could not be distinguished, but the melody was most beautiful. Finally it died away, and I determined to make one more cast and then return to the city "by moonlight alone," in my sail boat.

WILL BACK UP HIS STORY.

At this time I was using mossbunkers for bait, and making a long cast beyond the rocks was rewarded by a vigorous strike, but the subsequent play was unlike anything I had ever experienced. There was a downward rush, followed by a rise to the surface, and a fierce splashing, and something like a low moan came to my ears, while a pale face seemed to appear above the waves, weird and ghost-like. As this apparition sank from sight the struggle was renewed, and with my heart beating like a trip hammer, I strained the rod and line until at length the spectre, for thus it seemed to be, reappeared close to the rock on which I stood.

I staggered and fell, knocking out one of my teeth on a projecting crag, and at the same instant the hook was torn loose, and the mermaid, as I now discovered it to be, splashed back into the waves and disappeared. On the flat rock where the hook fell was the only memento of my strange fishing contest, a pearly white tooth, which I have had carefully polished and formed into the scarf pin that has so often excited the curiosity and admiration of my friends.

CHASED BY TIPSY FISH.

The railway men of the Northwest give glowing accounts of the superb fishing in that section, but you should participate in the fishing to be had in the South to know the pleasures of genuine angling, said Mr.

F. P. Reed, of the Monon Route. It is the custom among certain planters down in Alabama, and on the Gulf coast, to bait deep holes and attract immense numbers of game fish, which are then caught by set lines. Angle worms are often used, but Mr. Moonshine, who runs an illicit distillery down there, gathered a large quantity of the small spiral still-worms, and scattered them broadcast in the river near his home. With the worms was quite a quantity of worked-out mash from the distillery.

The next morning on visiting the place, he found the river in terrible commotion. A desperate, half-drunken conflict was going on between the catfish, eels, pike, sharks and almost every other variety of fish known to these waters. Mr. Moonshine fired several shots into the thickest of the fray, when he was instantly attacked by the catfish, gars and other vicious fish, and chased across the swamp to his own gate. The fright and nervous shock so prostrated him that he made application for a pass to Wisconsin or to Michigan, or to any northern state, where he could recuperate and be free from the voracious attacks of fish.

I have heard that northern railway officials, jealous of our reputation for unequaled fishing resorts, claimed that the man was chased by revenue officers instead of fish, but the plain, unvarnished tale as it was told to me by the planter was worth all the transportation we gave him.

SCIENTIFIC CAT FISHING.

Did you ever see a cat fish? inquired Mr. Grover Cleveland, of Washington, D. C. I do not mean the ordinary catfish of the waters, but a cat that will catch fish. Some years ago I was the proud possessor of a cat that supplied the family table with trout, black bass, and other game fish, during the proper season. This cat took to fishing as naturally as a duck takes to water. Just at dusk our fishing cat would go down to the river, and after first cap-tying a grasshopper would carefully crawl out on a half submerged log, and throw the bait perhaps two feet up stream. If a fish rose the cat would immediately seize it, using his strong talons after the style of the famous eagle-claw, which was used so successfully for fishing in years gone by.

The cat seldom failed to retain his hold on a fish, and would drag it along over the water to the shore in quite a scientific manner. After having the benefit of two years' experience, the cat learned to select the best natural bait, sometimes using frogs, and at other times grasshoppers or large houseflies, and I have always regarded the sagacity and skill of that feline angler with much admiration. I could never make the cat fish for catfish, but he was a keen angler for game fish.

A GRIZZLY COMBAT.

"The yarns that the hunters were spinning,
While the anglers were spinning their reels,
Could not be considered as sinning,
Though they lacked the magistrates' seals."

Speaking of athletic feats, said Mr. Ensign, of the National Advertising Agency, New York, I recall a little incident that occurred during my hunting experience in the Wild West. I was after grizzlies, and ordinarily had both my wits and my weapons about me, but this time, by singular neglect, I started a short distance from the spot where my rifle and hunting knife had been laid, and approaching a thicket was confronted by the largest grizzly bear it was ever my good fortune to meet. I had neither time nor inclination to run, as my coolness, courage and strength were such that I felt myself the equal of any wild beast west of the Rocky Mountains. The bear made a savage stroke at me with his paw, but only succeeded in knocking off my hat, whereupon he performed the scalp dance in a somewhat amusing manner, imagining, perhaps, that he had removed the upper section of my skull.

The battle which ensued was more exciting than any in which the celebrated "Grizzly Adams" ever participated. Having no weapons except those with which nature had provided me, I was at a disadvantage in regard to size and strength, but equalized matters by my activity and science. The bear evidently desired a contest of the "catch-as-catch-can" order, but I would not accommodate him. I parried and cleverly avoided every rush and stroke, and in turn dealt old Ephraim a number of fierce blows over the heart which staggered him, and finally killed the monster by a fierce upper cut, which broke his jaw and dislocated his neck. Strange as it may seem, I escaped without a scratch, though somewhat exhausted, and had the battle continued much longer, I really believe I might have been slightly injured. The bear's head has been tastefully mounted, and adorns a shield at my home, as proof of the accuracy of my story.

TALE OF A TIGER.

Tiger hunting is very dangerous sport, remarked Mr. John J. Byrne, of the Sante Fé Road, in his usual quiet and unassuming manner. Some ten years ago, while hunting in India, I had an experience which was more thrilling than usual. I had left my rifle in camp and started for a spring near at hand, when suddenly an immense tiger sprang at me, and I avoided him only by my remarkable activity. I was not at all frightened, and on the contrary, was very angry both at the audacity of the tiger, and at my own neglect in failing to carry my rifle.

As I could not fight his Royal Bengal Highness single-handed, there was nothing to do but to run, and I flatter myself there was an exhibition of speed which has not been equalled before or since by any professional athlete. At his first leap, the tiger barely missed me, tearing a fragment from my hunting coat. We were so evenly matched in speed that at every step I made down the trail through the jungle the tiger dropped in my footsteps, scratching my hunting boots at each bound. This race was continued for ten miles without any advantage being gained on either side, and I finally escaped by leaping a chasm too broad for the tiger to follow.

My anger and excitement by this time were at the boiling point, and the effect was to change the color of my hair from raven blackness to a fiery red, which color it remained for three years. I still keep the hunting boots, and can prove the truth of my story by the marks of the tiger's claws.

FANCY SHOOTING.

My modesty alone has prevented me taking championship honors in the way of fancy shooting, both with rifle and shot gun, said Mr. Geo. G. Po[illegible]ing, of New Haven. As proof of my skill with these weapons, I will mention a few feats which I frequently perform with great ease. One of my favorite recreations is duck shooting from a blind. In this sport I use nothing but a repeating rifle, and always shoot the incomers with such precision that the birds fall into the open game bag at my side. I invariably shoot the birds through the head, and on one occasion brought down five in succession from a flock passing overhead, much to the surprise of my companion as he saw one after another falling into the game bag.

Many years ago, when comparatively a novice, I used the shot gun, and by a peculiar system of loading, I charged the shells in such a manner that the shot instead of making the usual pattern would fly in any way I desired. For instance, in wild-goose shooting, the shot, at a distance of 50 to 75 or 100 yards, would fly in the form of a V, and in this manner I have killed a dozen wild geese at one time, each bird being shot through the head by a single pellet. That soon became tame sport, however, as it required little skill except in loading, and I now prefer the rifle for all kinds of wing shooting, and at all distances, even up to half a mile, at which altitude I have frequently brought down small birds barely visible to the naked eye.

A TERRIBLE ENCOUNTER.

While voyaging down the Mississippi last summer, said Mr. Ben Jefferson, of Lyon & Healy, Chicago, I had a rather peculiar adventure. I had camped for the night not far from the river, and lying beside the camp-fire was preparing for a good night's rest. Finally a strange sensation came over me, as of some threatening danger, and an instant later a terrible scream, evidently from a panther, sounded in my ears. The monster was immediately above me, judging from the sound, and as I glanced upward I saw his eyes blazing like balls of fire, evidently in anticipation of a feast upon my body. I seemed powerless to move, either fascinated or appalled by the sight, and my next sensation was one of pain, as I felt the talons of the beast at my head and throat. Exerting every energy, I threw the monster from me, and as I did so another fiendish scream rent the air. A slight explosion followed immediately after, and I saw, as I awoke from my troubled sleep, that a spark from the camp-fire had fallen into a percussion cap beneath the screech owl, which I had thrown violently from its perch upon my head. The force of the exploded percussion cap was sufficient to kill my terrible tormentor.

ZIGZAG RIFLE SHOOTING.

My proficiency in billiard playing aided me wonderfully in mastering the art of rifle shooting, said the quiet man, Mr. Frank Cheney, of Toledo. Not the mere rudiments of the art, as in simply hitting the bull's-eye at a reasonable distance, but in making caroms, so to speak. I deem it very easy for any man with steady nerves and a clear eye to make a straight score with a rifle at a thousand yards distance, and therefore I determined to be the originator of a new phase of rifle practice.

Beginning by the simple practice of "barking" squirrels, I gradually developed in skill until I could hit a ten cent piece a hundred yards distant —not aiming at the mark, but at a hardwood tree situated at right angles to the target. The bullet would glance from this to the edge of another tree and so on, in a semi-circle, until it reached the desired point. Perhaps the most difficult feat is to make the bullet take a zigzag course, first to the right, and then to the left, with a flight as irregular as a rail fence. To show you what may be done in this way, I will merely say that I once killed ten blackbirds at one rifle shot, the birds being diagonally opposite, on both sides of a wood road through the forest, and so accurate was my aim and estimate that with the small 22 caliber rifle bullet the plumage was not touched, the eyes only being shot out.

THE LAST BUFFALO HUNT.

Mr. John Jenkins, of Kansas City, who had been softly playing a Harvard guitar, and listening to the stories, put in his lingual oar at this juncture. Some ten years ago important business took me to the Northwest, where I remained several months, and devoted my leisure time to field sports. Buffalo were then abundant, and on several occasions I had good sport in their pursuit. Finally I decided upon an original plan, principally for the sake of novelty, and at once put it into execution. Taking the entire skin of a freshly-killed buffalo, with the head and horns complete, I prepared a framework in the department of the interior within which I could conceal myself, and by walking upon my hands and feet closely imitate the appearance and movements of the bison.

Noticing a large herd moving toward the river, one fine morning, I carefully approached, having previously prepared a half dozen revolvers within the framework of my dummy buffalo, the muzzle of each revolver just penetrating through the skin, and firmly fastened inside, with strings attached to the triggers. The herd was moving quite rapidly, and I stationed myself directly in their course, intending to fire a broadside and stampede the animals. At the first round, however, the herd instead of scattering pressed on more swiftly toward the river, and in a moment I found myself in the center of a vast throng of maddened animals, parched with thirst and eager to reach the water.

Escape was impossible for me, but fortunately the ranks pressed so closely together that I was carried along by the force of the moving body, as by an avalanche. I fired several fusilades from the revolvers as the herd shifted, changing my position toward the rear, as the infuriated animals crowded past me. Apparently the shots were without effect. To my horror, I soon observed that the course of the herd diverted from their original course, was directly toward an immense cliff overlooking the river, but I was unable to extricate myself. The strong framework about me prevented instant death from the crushing force on either side. Within a moment, as it seemed to me, I found myself upon the verge of the precipice, and was forced headlong into the stream amid the falling bodies of thousands of buffalo. The structure which I had prepared was airtight, except the apertures I had made through which I could breathe; therefore, while the animals floundered and many of them were drowned in the stampede, I floated down the stream and over the falls a short distance below the cliff. Drifting near shore, upon a sandbar, I was enabled to drag myself upon the bank where I lay for a short time exhausted.

Upon glancing toward the river I saw that it was full of the dead bodies of buffalo, and what was more surprising, all of my shots must have taken deadly effect, as the current was red with blood. From that day to this, the stream has been known as the Red River of the North, and the last herd of buffalo was exterminated, greatly to my regret, in this singular hunt which I had originated.

A WONDERFUL LIFE PRESERVER.

Hunters, like cats, should have nine lives in order to safely undergo all the perils of out-door adventure, remarked Mr. Upton, of the Oxford Manufacturing Company, Chicago. This idea was suggested to me by the fact that once in my "checkered career" a single shot from my rifle, at a critical moment, saved my life at least five times. It happened in this way. I was standing close to a craggy cliff, in a fine game region, with my rifle in hand, when all at once a startled elk, running along the base of the mountain, bounded almost upon me.

To avoid being trampled on, I leaped backward, firing the rifle at the same instant, and to my surprise, as I fell, I heard a death yell, evidently from an Indian some distance to my right. At the same instant the ground upon which I had just stood crumbled and fell, opening a chasm at least a hundred feet in depth, into which I would have been precipitated had I remained there an instant longer. The falling of this section of ground loosened a huge crag directly overhead, which dropped with terrible force into the abyss, so that if I had by any chance escaped instant death, I would have been crushed by the descending rock.

The elk, as I afterward found, had been struck by the bullet at the top of his skull, stunning him, and as he fell forward his antlers pierced a large rattlesnake, which was coiled ready to spring upon me at the point where I had formerly stood. The death-cry which I heard was from an Indian who had "drawn a bead" on me, and would doubtless have fired a fatal shot had it not been for my bullet which glanced from the head of the elk and struck the chief directly in the heart. This I have always considered a miraculous escape, and a hunting adventure somewhat unique in character.

AN INSATIATE ARCHER.

My favorite amusement is archery, in fact, my friends sometimes tell me that I "draw the long bow" too often, remarked Mr. Stanley Day, of New Market, N. J. It is astonishing to note the skill which may be attained by careful practice with the bow and arrow. I find it very easy to kill birds on the wing, and frequently by the use of three arrows have killed as many birds at one time. I also do curved shooting, using generally two arrows; each of the arrows has a curve, and will turn in a half circle, one to the right and the other to the left.

I have become quite an adept in this style of shooting, and can hit two bull's-eyes, each one hundred yards distant, and in exactly opposite directions. This would seem to be a difficult feat, but I accomplish the act by standing midway between the two, and shooting out at right angles, aiming by intuition, and seldom fail to strike the exact center of each target.

Once I adjusted the two arrows so carefully that in making a new experiment each of the projectiles in its flight covered a complete semicircle, and met fifty yards behind me, the steel points of the arrow heads becoming firmly fastened together. This I consider one of the most difficult and scientific performances ever recorded in the line of archery.

NEW JERSEY SNIPE SHOOTING.

My initiation as a snipe shooter over in New Jersey was a memorable event in my sporting career, soliloquized Senator Cornish, the organ manufacturer of Washington, New Jersey, who seemed to be communing with himself rather than speaking to the club members in the room. I was fresh from the prairies of the West, and knew nothing of shore or sea shooting in the vicinity of Gotham. One of my new found friends informed me, confidentially, that the summer flight of snipe was at its best on the Jersey marshes, and advised me to take a day off to try the sport. Accordingly I boarded an early train, engaged a native Jerseyman as guide and companion, and in less than an hour was on the historic snipe grounds at Pine Brook, made famous by Frank Forester.

My preconceived notions of snipe shooting seemed to be entirely wrong. The Jersey birds did not fly up and away in a zigzag course, with a "scaipe !" "scaipe !" as I had always supposed would be the regular order of things. These snipe just buzzed up around and toward me from every direction, and my breech-loader was kept hot by the repeated firing. Never since the celebrated blaze at Barnegat had such a single-handed fusilade occurred on the clinging soil of New Jersey. I killed an immense number of birds, and finally stopped after exhausting the ammunition and myself. My genial guide had bagged the snipe, and he laughed long and loud as he retrieved them for me, and witnessed my skill as a sportsman.

Finally, when I came to examine the wonderful bunch of birds I found it had shrunk in size, and consisted mainly of gauzy wings and long bills—in fact, Jersey mosquitoes! I added another bill (denomination V) to the pile, handed it to my companion, and as a parting act of politeness gave him my pocket pistol, heavily charged with double-distilled "Jersey lightning."

"The North for grayling, trout and bass,
The South for sea fish, and for tarpon;
The East for salmon, pike and bluefish,
And West for mountain trout to harp on."

For convenience in briefly describing the special angling attractions of various localities, the states north of the Ohio River will be included in the Northern group, those lying southward of that stream in the Southern section, the region east of Ohio will be considered the Eastern division, and west of the headwaters of the Missouri the Western portion.

NORTHERN STATES.

The grayling fishing of Michigan, as enjoyed on the Au Sable, the Hersey and Manistee Rivers, is a branch of angling not to be had elsewhere in any portion of the United States, except Montana. Information with regard to the best localities, etc., may be obtained by addressing Mr. Chas. S. Hampton, Petoskey, Mich.

For brook-trout fishing, Wisconsin, Michigan and Minnesota are the principal states in the North. Among the best localities are those near Ashland, Bayfield, Noquebay, Sparta and Westfield, Wis.; Cheboygan, Gogebic, Sault Ste. Marie, and Watersmeet, Mich.; Frontenac, Duluth, and Brule, Minn. For information concerning brook-trout fishing in these states, the reader may address Hon. S. S. Fifeld, Ashland, Wis., W. D. Tomlin, Duluth, Minn., or Mr. E. E. Thresher, Kalamazoo, Mich.

Black bass are quite abundant in the lakes and streams of most of the Northern States. Good fishing waters are near Huron, Sandusky, and Tiffin, Ohio; Angola, Elkhart, and Pleasant Lake, Ind; Aroma, Kankakee, and Waukegan, Ill; Buena Vista, Okoboji, and Spirit Lake, Iowa;

Bowling Green, Rock Castle Springs, and Williamsburg, Ky.; Eldorado, Eureka, and Parsons, Kan; Allegan, Battle Creek, Coldwater, Elk-Rapids, Gogebic, Petoskey, and Sturgis, Mich; Alexandria, Big Lake, and Lake Pepin, Minn.; Jamestown, Wahpeton, and Thompson, N. Dak.; Columbus, Duncan, and Waterloo, Neb.; Big Stone City, Dell Rapids, and Wilmot, S. Dak.; Eagle River, Florence, Montello, Oconomowoc, Sheboygan Falls, and Summit Lake, Wis.

Mascalonge fishing is excellent in the vicinity of Detroit, Glenwood, Little Falls, Prior Lake, and Staples Mill, Minn.; Alanson, Mackinac Island, Sault Ste. Marie, and Seney, Mich.; Butternut, Eagle River, Fifield, Phillips, Woodruff, and Pelican, Wis.

For pike, pickerel, perch, and small bass, the angler may select almost any of the lakes and rivers in the states mentioned, and be reasonably sure of good fishing.

Accurate information in regard to localities, best seasons, etc., in these states may be had by enclosing self-addressed, stamped envelope to one of the following anglers: Col. W. T. Dennis, Richmond, Ind; Dr. S. P. Bartlett, Quincy, Ill.; C. F. Bates, Cedar Rapids, Iowa; Geo. A. Johnson, Detroit, Mich.; Hon. W. David Tomlin, Duluth, Minn.; Dr. James A. Rankin, Jamestown, N. Dak.; Dr. James A. Henshall, Cincinnati, Ohio; J. N. Wass, Beresford, S. Dak.; Geo. F. Peabody, Appleton, Wis.

SOUTHERN STATES.

Tarpon fishing—for which the waters of the southern coast are most widely celebrated—may be had at its best along the shores of Florida. Several of the prominent resorts are on the gulf coast, in the vicinity of Apalachicola, Cedar Keys, Punta Rassa, Homosassa, Pensacola, Tampa, Charlotte Harbor, Tarpon Springs, and Naples. The tarpon is also found along the coast of Louisiana and Texas, where it is known, locally, as the "Grand Ecaille" (pronounced "grandykye," and signifying large scale fish), and in some fishing towns it is termed the "savonilla."

Other popular sea fishes—notably the Spanish mackerel, sheepshead, sea bass, etc.—are caught in abundance near Mobile, Ala.; Braidentown, Cedar Keys, Indian River, Jacksonville, Key West, New Smyrna, Pensacola, and St. Augustine, Fla.; Brunswick, Darien, and Savannah, Ga.; New Orleans, La.; Mississippi City, Miss.; New Berne, Rodanthe, and Wilmington, N. C.; Charleston, Georgetown, and Coosawhatchie, S. C.; Chincoteague, Hampton Roads, Norfolk, and Phœbus, Va.

The fresh water fishing is excellent in many portions of the Southern States, the principal varieties of fish being black bass, perch, pike, mullet, and occasionally trout. A few of the favorite angling resorts are: Broken Arrow, Decatur, Eutaw, and Wetumpka, Ala.; Corning, Eureka Springs, Pine Bluff, and Van Buren, Ark.; Cantonment, Enterprise, and Kissimee, Fla.; Acworthy, Calhoun, and Powersville, Ga.; Vinita, Ind. Ter.; Bowling Green, Rock Castle Springs, and Williamsburgh, Ky.; Raceland, and Washington, La.; Hagerstown, Oakland, and Seven Locks, Md.; Crocker, Jerome, New Florence, and Missouri City, Mo.; Chama, Espanola, and Fort Stanton, New Mex.; Clyde, Pigeon River, and Sylva, N. C.; Gourdins, Kingston, and Scranton, S. C.; Boyce, Huntington, Manchester, Reelfoot Lake, and Waverly, Tenn.; Kountze, La Coste, and Waelder, Tex.; Lexington, Riverton, and Wytheville, Va.; Berkeley Springs, Harper's Ferry, and Sleepy Creek, W. Va.

References: J. H. Hardaway, Montgomery, Ala.; Col. J. A. Woodson, Little Rock, Ark.; J. Mortimer Murphy, Sponge Harbor, Fla.; Harry C. Brown, Atlanta, Ga., Harry L. Means, Louisville, Ky.; Col. J. R. Thornton, Alexandria, La.; J. A. Hartner, Orangeville, Md.; Geo. J. Chapman, 720 Pine Street, St. Louis, Mo.; J. Minium, E. Las Vegas, New Mex.; Edw. S. Latimer, Wilmington, N. C.; V. O. Hendrick, Huntingdon, Tenn.; J. B. Gilbert, Houston, Tex.; W. M. Williams, Richmond, Va.

EASTERN STATES.

Bluefish and striped bass fishing take first rank in the way of angling along the coast of the Eastern States—squidding or trolling for bluefish being a popular recreation in connection with sailing, and bass casting taking precedence over all other forms of sea fishing, among the scientific anglers whose principal pastime is with rod and line on the ocean tides from Cape May to Cape Cod.

For striped bass fishing a few of the popular resorts are near Milford, New London, Southport, and Stonington, Conn.; Buzzard's Bay, Cataumet, E. Marshfield, Fair Haven, and Woods Holl, Mass.; Newmarket and Portsmouth, N. H.; Barnegat, Elizabeth, Sewaren, and Tuckerton, N. J.; Canarsie, Mamaroneck, Giffords, Fort Hamilton, and Sheepshead Bay, N. Y.; Block Island (via New London), and Warren, R. I.

For bluefish, the resorts above named and many others on the Eastern and New England coast, from Delaware Bay to Penobscot Bay. The localities along the Atlantic coast, where bluefish, sheepshead, weakfish, kingfish, and other species of sea fish are abundant, within the range specified, are literally too numerous to mention.

Brook trout fishing of excellent quality may be enjoyed in the vicinity of Andover, Litchfield, and Shepang, Conn.; Middle Dam, Parmachenee Lake, Phillips, and Rangeley Lakes, Me.; Plymouth, Renfrew, Shelburne Falls, and Westfield, Mass.; Gorham, Laconia, and Salmon Falls, N. H.; Dunnfield, Oak Ridge, and Vernon, N. J.; Alder Creek, Ausable, Adirondack, Big Indian, Boonville, Callicoon, Canisteo, Deposit, and Wellsville, N. Y.; Dingman's Ferry, Oakland, Shohola, Westfield, and White Haven, Pa.; Abbott's Run, Greene, and Washington, R. I.; Bellow's Falls, Morrisville, Summit, and Wolcott, Vt.

Black bass are abundant near Chopinville, Litchfield, and Winsted, Conn.; Belgrade, Fryeburg, and Highland Lake, Me.; Milford, Southbridge, and West Acton, Mass.; Alton, Centre Conway, and Nashua, N. H.; Dover, Lake Hopatcong, and Weston, N. J.; Binghamton, Canaan, Clayton, Dunkirk, Greenwood Lake, Lockport, Oswego, and Westport, N. Y.; Erie, Freemansburg, Lackawaxen, Tunkhannock, and West Conshohocken, Pa.; Charlston, and River Point, R. I.; Back Bay, Bellows Falls, Ludlow, and Sheldon, Vt.

For mascalonge a few of the favorite Eastern localities are Clayton, Ogdensburg, and Theresa, N. Y.; Barton, and Newport, Vt. Other varieties of fresh-water fish, *i. e.*, pike, pickerel, perch, etc., are plentiful in many lakes and streams throughout the Eastern States.

References: Dr. E. P. Gregory, Waterbury, Conn.; Edward M. Blanding, Bangor, Me.; Walter M. Brackett, 41 Tremont St., Boston, Mass.; Geo. C. Gilmore, Manchester, N. H.; Robert D. Foote, Morristown, N. J.; Wakeman Holberton, 18 Vesey St., New York City, N. Y.; A. B. Shipley & Son, Philadelphia, Pa.; Chas F. Orvis, Manchester, Vt.

WESTERN STATES.

Plentifully distributed over that vast area of country generally known as the "Far West," are thousands of rivers, lakes and brooks filled with some of the finest game fish in America. A few of the excellent fishing localities are enumerated in the following list:

For brook trout, rainbow trout, and mountain trout, Belmont, Chico, Clairville, Fulton, Lone Pine, Monterey, Redwood City, San Mateo, Soledad, and Windsor, Cal.; Boulder, Breckenridge, Buena Vista, Cimarron, Delta, Golden, Gunnison, Idaho Springs, Longmont, Montrose, St. Elmo, and Villa Grove, Colo.; Camas, Eagle Rock, Inkom, Rathdrum, Sand Point, and Shoshone, Idaho; Avon, Billings, Butte, Custer, Elliston, Gallatin, Garrison, Heron, Livingston, Park City, Ravalli, Red Rock, Stillwater and Woodlin, Mont.; Carson and Palisade, Nev.; Albany, Corvallis, Oregon City, and Salem, Ore.; Clear Creek, Milford, Ogden, Richmond, Smithfield, and Thistle, Utah; Carbonado, Cascades, Lake View, Olympia, and Waitsburg, Wash.; Carter, Fort Washakie, Hilliard, Piedmont, and Twin Creek, Wyo.

For salmon fishing and sea fish, the following points are excellent: Monterey and Windsor, Cal.; Astoria, Bonneville, Columbia, and Oregon City, Ore.; Alderton, Cascades, Olympia, and Seattle, Wash. In the fresh waters, inland, game fish are abundant from the Rocky mountains to the Pacific coast.

References: Harry Babcock, 306 California St., San Francisco, Cal.; Hon. L. B. France, Denver, Colo.; Chas. Nathurst, Sappington, Mont.; Hon. S. H. Greene, 204 Stark St., Portland, Ore.; W. J. Dermody, Ogden, Utah; E. E. Ellis, 903 Pacific Ave., Tacoma, Wash.

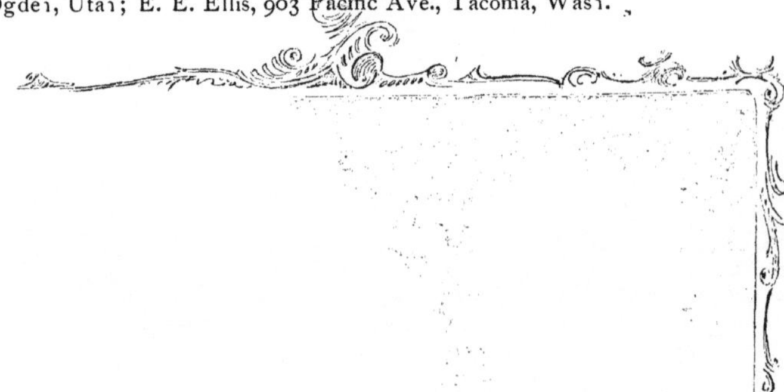

BLUEFISHING.

MONTHLY FISHING GUIDE.

"Mark well the various seasons of the year,
When the successive fishing months appear;
In each revolving moon some fish there be
That may be taken in river or in sea."

JANUARY.

For the majority of anglers January represents the "winter of discontent," so far as fishing is concerned. Florida, the perennial paradise of the angling brotherhood, yields good sport at this period of the year, when the bluefish, Spanish mackerel, sheepshead, groupers, and other varieties of sea-fish bite well at the favorite resorts, named elsewhere. On the Gulf coast of Texas, Louisiana, Mississippi and Alabama, the fishing is also good during January.

FEBRUARY.

The month of February is considered—by the fishing fraternity—much more welcome than its predecessor. It is three days shorter than January, and one month nearer to the general season of piscatorial pleasures. Winter fishing through the ice can of course be indulged in by Northern rodsters, but that is a rather "chill and cheerless pastime" to most men. Aside from this amusement there is none with rod and line in the North, and the good fishing of the Gulf coast has one disheartening feature for multitudes of anglers—it is too far away.

MARCH.

To the lover of angling, as also to the soldier, the word "March!" signifies something. To the former it means a step nearer, on the calendar, toward the longed-for fishing season. The tarpon fisher greets it as the time of the preliminary skirmish with his favorite finny adversary, and the sea-fishing of Florida is good. On the whole, there is something breezy about March, and "It's an ill wind that profits nobody."

APRIL.

April showers do something more than "bring forth May flowers." They bring forth those early croakers, the frogs, telling in hoarse yet happy voices to the world in general and anglers in particular the glad tidings that the Spring rise is in the brooks and the trout are rising too. In most of the states trouting begins in this variable, vernal month, and it is held in high esteem accordingly.

MAY.

May is the month pre-eminently intended for and dedicated to the disciples of Izaak Walton. It seems to be universally accepted by the fraternity as the brightest, best and balmiest of the twelve changeful cycles of the year. Local or special restrictions excepted, brook trout may be legally taken in most of the states and territories. May is distinguished, also as being probably the best for tarpon fishing in southern waters. It is the time when a majority of anglers feel a keen desire to "fight it out on this line if it takes all summer."

JUNE.

June may be termed the month of the salmon, although it is almost equally famous as the month of the black bass, which are in season and rise readily to the artificial fly in most sections at this period. The tarpon fishing is also in its prime, and mascalonge fishing of the finest kind may be had in the St. Lawrence River, about the Thousand Islands, and in the Northern states, particularly Wisconsin and Michigan. June is a favorite month for bluefishing along the Eastern coast.

JULY.

Patriotic anglers will find almost universal freedom to go a-fishing for any and all kinds of fish, and in all sections of the Union—except upon preserves, leased or purchased. Salmon, brook trout, mascalonge, black bass, pike, pickerel, etc., are all in season, ready to be taken by hook—but not by crook, except in the form of a gaff.

AUGUST.

During this month—and in many localities even during July—the waters of inland lakes, particularly through the pine land and wooded sections of country, are "in bloom," as it is technically called, the surface being covered with aquatic seeds and vegetation. In such localities, during this period, the bass, pickerel and mascalonge fishing is poor. Moreover, the angler receives so many bites, even when the fish are not to be found, that August is not a popular month in the calendar, except for sea fishing in the East.

SEPTEMBER.

Blithe September is a better month for sea-fishing than for angling in fresh waters—the season for brook-trout fishing having closed, in most states, with the end of August. For striped bass fishing off the New Jersey and Connecticut coast, September is a favorable period, and the bluefish, sheepshead, weakfish, etc., also bite well at this time.

OCTOBER.

The month of October is more favorable for the gun than for the rod in the Northern states, though persistent anglers making their annual farewell casts, either in the ocean surf or the lakes and streams, occasionally make fair catches. The banging of the breech-loader, however, takes the place of the humming of the reel to a great extent.

NOVEMBER.

With the beginning of November the better varieties of game fish in the sea having departed southward for their winter sojourn, and the mascalonge, pike, pickerel and perch,—the only fresh water varieties available—feed principally in deep water, "on their own hook," instead of taking other hooks, no matter how temptingly offered.

DECEMBER.

For all practical purposes December is a "closed time" for fishing in the Northern, Eastern and Western states. The inland waters are usually closed by ice, and even when open the well-stocked lake or stream would, at this period, prove to be a veritable "slough of despond" for scientific angling. Any wise Horace of the present time would vary the familiar advice given by the late sage of the *Tribune*, and say to the December angling enthusiast: "Go South, young man, go South!"

GAME AND SHOOTING.

"While thousands are doomed every
  moment to yield
To business or studies severe,
The sportsman enjoys the pure air
  of the field,
And roams without sorrow or fear;
He sighs not for honor, for splendor, or wealth,
Better blessings than either attend him,
Behold, on his brow sit contentment and health,
And the dictates of conscience befriend him."

The sportsmen of America have for many generations past enjoyed a greater variety of field sports than could be found in any other civilized country. So numerous, in fact, were the varieties of game, and so apparently inexhaustible the supply, that few restrictions were placed upon the shooters, and in consequence of this the country has been for fifty years past overrun by not only the native lovers of field sports, and market gunners, but sportsmen of foreign lands have swelled the throngs to exterminate several of the valued species of game—birds and animals.

During the first half of the present century the native American, even though his worldly possessions consisted of merely a simple shooting outfit, could obtain, comparatively without cost, better sport than European princes could boast of in their own country. The United States in reality seemed to furnish a sort of Happy Hunting Ground for the sportsmen of our own land and the wealthy shooters of European countries. All this, however, has sadly changed during the past twenty-five years. The bison or buffalo, which formerly roamed over the broad plains beyond the Mississippi in countless numbers, now exists (on the public domains) only within the limits of Yellowstone Park, where a small band of two or three hundred has been preserved, though a few wanton hide hunters have, during the past winter, attempted to destroy the last remnant of this distinctive species of American game.

The destruction of the buffalo is but an indication of the coming fate of the moose, the elk, and other valuable species of game, unless strict protective laws are enacted and enforced. Unfortunately, the propagation of game can not be successfully undertaken on a large scale for the public benefit, as is done with the better varieties of American game fish. Twenty years ago the annual flight of the migratory pigeons darkened the air in spring-time, but at present the species seems to be practically annihilated. This result has been reached by indiscriminate slaughter, principally for the markets and for trap-shooting tournaments.

It will be seen that while American sportsmen have been blessed with privileges and opportunities in the line of field sports equalled by no other nation, the time is not far distant when none but wealthy sportsmen, or clubs owning large game preserves, can hope to find good sport in any of the states, except perhaps those bordering on the Pacific Coast. The

destruction of American field sports for the common masses would be felt as a national calamity, as the proper indulgence of the passion for out-door recreation has done much to foster and maintain the spirit of independence, the manly vigor and remarkable courage, which is recognized as a characteristic of native-born Americans. With the gradual passing away of a love for or opportunity to indulge in field sports, there springs into existance the passion for more debasing pastimes, as indicated particularly in many of the large cities and their vicinity, where gambling, pugilism, and other so-called sports too often take the place of honorable out-door recreation, to a certain degree.

A careful historian once asserted, giving ample proof for the statement, that modern nations excelled in arts, sciences, and agriculture, as well as in other vocations of peace and war, in proportion as the young men exhibited a tendency to indulge in the sports of shooting, fishing and other manly amusements of the field. Upon the sportsmen of America, therefore, devolves the duty of maintaining for future generations the supply of game birds and animals, which have, in the past, been so recklessly destroyed without thought of future consequence. Public sentiment has been aroused against the wanton slaughter of game, and it is believed that the efforts of local clubs and state organizations formed to enforce the game and fish laws will have the effect of preventing the extermination of valuable species, particularly in view of the fact that a strong National Game, Bird, and Fish Protective Association has been organized, during the past year, to co-operate with local associations in this direction.

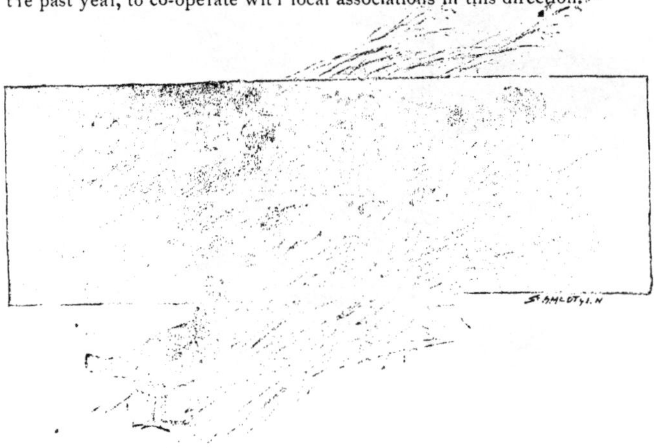

"In the far-away northernmost wilds of Maine,
Where the murmuring pines all the year complain,
In the unknown Aroostook's lonesome world,
Or where the waters of Moosehead are curl'd,
The stalwart wood-cutter spreads his camp,
In his cabin of logs trims his winter lamp:
And many a savory banquet doth cheer,
The fireside joys of his wintry year,
With haunch of moose and the dappled deer."

THE MOOSE.

The moose is the largest, as well as the most highly prized species of the deer family to be found within the limits of the United States. Formerly this species was very abundant throughout the region of country extending from the wilds of northern Maine westward through the wilderness bordering on the Great Lakes and far beyond, but great havoc has been wrought, especially during the past twenty-five years, in the supply of this variety of game. Comparatively few are killed annually in the United States, and these mostly within the limits of northern Maine and the states of the far Northwest; where the pernicious activity of professional hunters and self-styled sportsmen, who kill the large beasts during the prevalence of deep snows, will, if not checked, bring the moose into the list of extinct species of American game before the close of another decade.

In appearance the moose is large and awkward; its huge head and broad nose, combined with its short, thick neck, giving it a rather grotesque look. The moose travels over the ground with remarkable speed, not after the style of the common deer, with long graceful bounds, but in a swinging trot, crashing through the thickets and over fallen logs, with a noise that may be heard quite a distance. This style of locomotion is adopted only when the animal is suddenly startled. If the presence of man is detected by the wary animal while the hunter is yet some distance away, the moose moves off with the greatest caution, often selecting a course which the follower can pursue only with the greatest difficulty. The endurance of the animal is such that only the hardiest of hunters can hope to overtake him in a stern chase, when he has once been alarmed. The broad, palmate antlers of the moose are a distinguishing feature, and happy is the hunter who can boast the possession of a head as a trophy taken from an animal killed by himself.

Still-hunting or stalking the moose in his native wilds is a branch of sport successfully followed by none except the skilled woodsman and hardy hunter. The fatigue and countless obstacles to be met with are such that comparatively few amateur sportsmen attempt it. More frequently the animal is driven to water by the guides and woodsmen, or attracted to such localities by calling. The call is made by imitating the plaintive low of the cow moose, or if required, the bellow of the bull moose. A trumpet of birch bark is used, and if the call is properly made and carefully repeated at intervals, it will seldom fail to bring the moose within range of the hunter's rifle.

In northern Maine and in the Canadian Provinces, the moose is often hunted during early winter by pursuing him on snowshoes. Fire hunting, which consists in using a jack-lamp or torchlight, is often effectively followed in midsummer, along the lakes and rivers. This method of shining is not considered very sportsmanlike by those who possess the requisite skill and endurance to adopt the style of still hunting. In Professor Meyer's entertaining work, entitled "Sport with Gun and Rod," will be found two instructive articles on moose hunting — one by the Earl of Dunraven, the other by Mr. Charles C. Ward, a practical sportsman and fine descriptive writer.

"Far from the cultivated realm
Where human labor fells the wood,
Cleaves the rich glebe and tills the soil,
Incessant toiling for its food,
The great elk of the wilderness,
Boon nature's noblest, fleetest child,
Since the creation hath possess'd
And rang'd, untamable, the waste,
Cropt the sweet grasses of the wild,
In savage freedom roam'd and rac'd."

THE ELK.

The American Elk, frequently called the Wapiti, is more handsome and graceful than the moose, though it does not equal the latter in size. In form the elk closely resembles the common deer, and in color it is of a yellowish brown; of a dark tinge in winter, and lighter in summer. The antlers or horns are more upright than in the common deer, and are very symmetrical. The range of the elk, which formerly extended over the greater portion of the United States, is now restricted principally to the far West. Beyond the Rocky Mountains, not many years ago, the elk could be found in bands sometimes several hundred in number, but at the present time it is rare to see a herd of more than fifty, even in favored localities in Wyoming and Montana. The great National Yellowstone Park has proved to be a haven of refuge for this variety of game, and it is believed by careful observers that quite a large percentage of the elk now roaming in the United States have their habitat in that natural game preserve. Mr. Hofer, an experienced guide and woodsman of the Yellowstone country, states that the elk migrate annually to quite a large extent, moving to the south and southwest to the warmer places late in autumn, and returning to the park when the heavy snows are melted in the spring. Still hunting is the method commonly employed in following the elk, though occasionally the animal is killed in open country by hunters on horseback. The bands of elk in the mountainous country frequent the highest hills, and on the plains they are to be found usually near the streams, in or near the thickets of willows.

Elk hunting is exciting sport, and if careful restrictive laws are enforced to prevent the extermination of the species it may be enjoyed within a limited area of country for many years to come.

THE VIRGINIA DEER.

"And there at their head, at brief advance,
I see a stately stag in career,
A stag that bounds, that struggles for life,
The proud, the hunted, the frantic deer."

The best known and most widely distributed species of the deer family in America is the common red deer, or Virginia deer, which is to be found at the present time in nearly every state of the Union. Although the common deer is by nature shy and timid, it does not wholly forsake the haunts of civilization, as proved by the fact that deer hunting is still a popular pastime in Pennsylvania, and New York state, in the wilderness and mountainous country not far from the large towns and agricultural districts.

Of the characteristics and methods of hunting this highly prized variety of game much has been written, but no better practical treatise exists than the admirable book entitled "The Still Hunter," by Mr. T. S. Van Dyke. Nearly half a century ago a most attractive little volume, "The Deer Stalkers," by Frank Forester, was published for the entertainment of American sportsmen and the work is still eagerly read, but in view of the fact that it is a sporting romance, with instruction as an incidental feature, it cannot in this latter respect bear comparison with the former volume.

Still hunting or deer stalking is by far the most prevalent and popular method of pursuit. In several states the use of hounds or any other kind of dogs is prohibited in deer hunting, as many believe that hounding practically drives the deer out of the section where the custom is common. In the Eastern states the favorite localities for deer hunting are in the

Adirondack region of northern New York, and the wilderness portion of Maine. Farther west deer are found in abundance, especially in the states bordering upon the British possessions.

In certain portions of the South, notably in Georgia, the time-honored sport of deer hunting with horse and hounds is followed to a considerable extent, but in most portions of the United States the character of the country is such that this sport cannot be successfully pursued. Under favorable conditions there can be no more exciting sport than this, and it is one which may be participated in by both sexes. In fact, some of the most enthusiastic followers of the chase in Georgia and Mississippi are ladies. This pastime has been thrillingly described by the late "Ellen Alice," and by another charming writer, "Beryl," a lady belonging to one of the first families of Georgia.

Fire hunting is a method which can not be endorsed, as it is successfully put in practice only during midsummer, when deer are driven to the lakes and rivers by the flies and winged pests, and the game at this season is not in proper condition. There is something unsportsmanlike in floating within a few yards of a dazed creature, and killing it by a shot as it stands half submerged in the water. The same objections hold good as applied to driving deer with hounds down to the lakes or streams in midsummer for the purpose of killing. A spirit of sportsmanship requires that some skill be displayed on the part of the hunter, and a fair opportunity for life given the hunted.

THE ANTELOPE.

"I'll chase the antelope over the plain,
And the tiger's cub I'll bind with a chain,
And the wild gazelle with its silvery feet,
I'll give to thee for a playmate sweet."

On the plains of the West a very popular and exciting sport is that of antelope hunting, either with the swift greyhounds and speedy horses, or by still hunting. The latter is a difficult method, as the antelope is a remarkably shy animal, except when its curiosity is aroused. It can sometimes be lured within range by the hunter lying in wait, concealed by a rock or some other object and waving a handkerchief. If the hunter is carefully concealed, and the taint of his presence is not borne to the delicate nostrils of the game, the antelope will approach nearer and nearer until within easy range, their curiosity overcoming their judgment.

When the hunter desires to approach the game by stalking, or still hunting, the greatest of caution is required, as he must approach his quarry unobserved, and in doing so it is often necessary to creep or crawl through the prairie grass for quite a distance.

Several other varieties of the deer family—the black tail deer, mule deer, etc.—furnish good sport to the hunters of the West, but the style of hunting does not differ materially from that employed in following the species already mentioned, therefore it is unnecessary to give a description of each. Judge Caton's practical work, "The Antelope and Deer of America," gives valuable instruction as to the haunts, habits and habitat of these game animals.

THE GRIZZLY BEAR.

" Mid scenes magnificently grand
In forest ground and mountain land,
Savage and solitary lord
Of dark ravine and pastures broad,
The grizzly bear, beyond the dome
Of Rocky Mountains, holds its home."

The spice of danger attending the sport of grizzly bear hunting gives it a peculiar claim to many who are fond of the wild sports of the West. It is a pastime requiring coolness and skill, and should not be attempted by any amateur who knows nothing of the habits and character of the animal. The haunts of this savage beast are in the rocky canyons and dense thickets among the mountains, where the hunter is liable to come upon it suddenly and unexpectedly. If he is not the possessor of rare courage, coolness and presence of mind, he may discover when too late that bear hunting has no attractions for him; in fact that he "has not lost any bear," and he did not wish to find any.

The principal danger is to amateurs or novices of this description. Experienced hunters are always prepared, and are seldom killed or seriously injured. The appearance of a grizzly bear, when angry, is sufficiently frightful to alarm and unnerve any excitable person. In size he is a monster, specimens having been killed weighing nearly 1000 pounds, and the open countenance of bruin with his murderous teeth could not be considered reassuring. The grizzly bear is most abundant west of the Rocky Mountains in the extreme northwestern states and territories, from Montana to Oregon, where he is usually at home to all comers who may desire to seek him persistently. The common black bear, less dangerous and more widely distributed, is sought by hunters in many sections of the country—being usually trailed and treed by dogs.

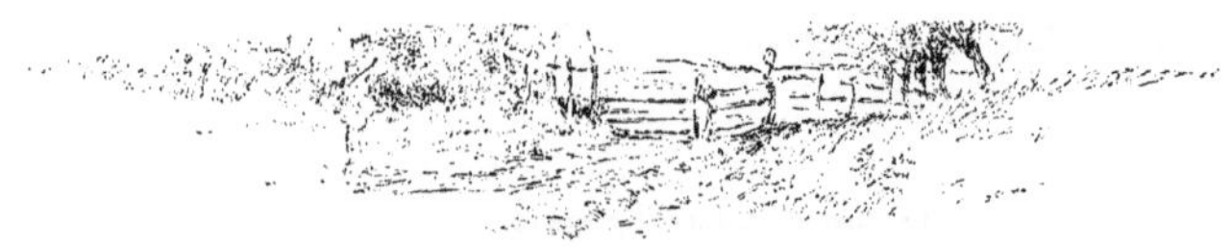

The mountain lion crouching sat,
Where prowl'd the lynx and fierce wild-cat;
O'er crags sprang mountain goats and sheep,
While hare and rabbits startled, leap.

OTHER FOUR-FOOTED GAME.

Along the mountain ranges near the Pacific coast the California lion, or mountain lion, an animal of great strength and activity, is quite frequently found by adventurous hunters, and the common wild-cat and lynx are found in many if not most of the large forest areas of the United States. These animals are seldom hunted as a specialty, or as affording a distinct branch of field sports, but their pursuit is exciting, and their killing is hailed with delight by frontiersmen, whose flocks and herds suffer from their depredations. The same is true of the wolf.

The Rocky Mountain goats and sheep—each species being now in process of extermination—are objects of interest to keen still hunters who possess the agility and endurance of Alpine crag climbers. Of the common hare, or rabbit, the late Col. F. G. Skinner has given entertaining testimony, through the sportsmen's journals, as to the capital sport which may be had by pursuing the "cotton tails" with well-trained beagles; and of the large jack-rabbit of the West it may be said to his credit that he has been the "prime mover"—in fact, always takes the lead in carrying on the sport of coursing upon American soil, and therefore "may his tribe increase."

"They come from frosty solitudes, where broods the Arctic night,
Where deserts grim, spread vast and dim, in the auroral light.
The Esquimaux, with bended bow, fast paddling his canoe,
Their flocks hath chas'd o'er icy waste of waters heavenly blue."

WATER-FOWL.

Most majestic of all American species of water-fowl is the great trumpeter swan, of pure white plumage, graceful in form and movement, large in size—attaining about twenty-five pounds weight—but so small in numbers that it will no doubt be recorded, ere long, as an extinct variety of game in the United States.

More numerous by far, yet still a rare visitant in most sections of the country—except the lake and river regions and the ocean coast—is the Canada goose, or common wild goose, considered a prize by all lovers of wild fowl shooting. The wild goose shooter, particularly in the West, usually ensconces himself snugly under concealment of a blind, and decoys (either live, domesticated-wild geese, or artificial figures) can be used to advantage in most sections. The brant, practically, may be regarded as a "small edition" of the wild goose.

The several species of ducks sought by wild-fowl shooters, rank in about the following order. First, the highly-prized canvas-back, a delicacy by reason of the wild celery upon which it feeds in the Chesapeake Bay, of the south, and Lake Koshkonong, of the north; then the red-head, closely resembling the canvas-back in size, appearance and habits; next

the mallard, the best known and most eagerly followed of inland wild ducks; and finally, the beautiful crested wood-duck, the widgeon, the pin-tail or spring-tail, the gadwall or gray duck, the green-winged and blue-winged teal, the buffel-head, the scaup duck, etc. Amateur sportsmen wishing to learn how, and when and where to enjoy sport in this line should consult Mr. W. B. Leffingwell's book entitled "Wild Fowl Shooting," a standard work on the subject.

WILD TURKEY.

"This wandering, shy, secluded bird,
This roamer of the forest-ground,
Thro' all the Western wilderness,
In dense, embowering haunt is found."

As a distinct American game bird of high quality,—closely related, through its ancestry, to the fine fowls "that the commissaries found" when the boys in blue were marching through Georgia—the wild turkey is deserving of distinguished consideration. The wild turkey is considerably larger than the domestic bird, and the adult male in his native haunts is one of the proudest and handsomest specimens of winged game to be found in the United States.

In the early part of the present century, when Daniel Boone was the pioneer hunter of the West, the habitat of the wild turkey extended northward into Illinois, Indiana, Ohio and the Northwestern states, but it is now found mainly in the South and Southwest. An expert caller, imitating the yelp of the wild turkey, can usually attract the wary birds within easy rifle range. Dogs are sometimes used in hunting wild turkeys, and the sport when pursued in any proper style is very enjoyable. Col. James Gordon ("Pious Jeems"), of Mississippi, an accomplished sportsman, and writer, is the author of several instructive essays on this subject.

PRAIRIE CHICKENS.

> "When August and September days
> Flush the broad prairies with their blaze,
> The young broods, now matur'd, expand
> Their wings and flutter o'er the land."

One hundred years ago the pinnated grouse, or prairie chicken, as it is generally termed, was comparatively abundant in the East, particularly on the brushy plains of Long Island, where it was known as the heath hen. Now, the prairie chicken is essentially a Western game bird, found in numbers only in the region beyond the Mississippi, the species having been exterminated in the East.

North and South Dakota cover probably the best region for prairie chicken shooting, and if the birds are properly protected during the close season, and non-export laws rigidly enforced, the land of the Dakotas' will furnish excellent recreation in this line for future generations. With well-trained setters or pointers, ranging fast and free over the broad prairie lands, where every movement of the dogs and the whirring flight of the birds can be carefully noted by the sportsman, pinnated grouse shooting stands well toward the front in the list of American field sports.

RUFFED GROUSE.

> "Where greenwood shadows shift and swim,
> As in cathedral arches dim,
> There the shy partridge loves to brood,
> Deep in the shelter of the wood."

This woodland hermit—the pheasant of the East, and partridge of the West—is a sort of country cousin of the pinnated grouse, or prairie chicken. In its haunts and habits the ruffed grouse is almost the opposite of his prairie relative. He seeks the secluded thickets and dense woods, and will seldom lie to the point of a dog, though a barking cur or "partridge dog" will frequently tree him, and enable the gunner to shoot him from a limb—a proceeding not properly to be classed as sport.

The ruffed grouse is swift of flight, and, when much pursued, is difficult to approach. The sportsman who can kill a large percentage of his birds on the wing, in thick cover such as the ruffed grouse frequents, may certainly take rank as a crack shot, whether in the wildwoods of Wisconsin or among the mountains of Maine.

Shooting Chickens at Edge of Westfield.

THE QUAIL.

> " Sweet now at morn and eve the quail
>   Repeats its plaintive, whistling note,
> And softly fall the answering cries
>   That over wood and corn-field float."

The common quail, diversely known in various sections as Bob White, Virginia partridge, and colin, is probably the most widely distributed of upland game birds in the country. Unlike most other species the quail dwells close to the farmer's home, and the whistle of "Bob White" is often heard around the barn and the stacks of grain, when the bevies are unmolested.

Many keen sportsmen regard the quail as the best representative game bird of America, and the various field trials—held annually to decide the merits of setters and pointers, in competition—are almost invariably conducted in localities where Bob White is the only game pursued to test the staunchness, nose, pace, style, and other working qualities of the dogs. The plumed quails of the Pacific coast—the valley quail and the mountain quail—are the most beautiful members of the happy family.

THE WOODCOCK.

> " Where scarce the sun-spears, quivering bright,
> May pierce the foliage with their light,
> Ah! there so shadowy sleeps the wood
> Where hermit woodcock seek their food."

A species of long bill that is honored on sight is the woodcock, boring in the moist meadows and dark forest grounds for his daily food, but never becoming a bore to the lover of field sports. In midsummer the first, the best, in fact the only game bird that may be legally killed is the woodcock. His flight from among the ferns or thickets is swift, almost noiseless, and J. Cypress, Jr., was correct in asserting that "to stop a woodcock in a thick brake, where you can see him only with the eye of faith, * * requires an eye, and a hand, and a heart, which science cannot manufacture."

The Warwick woodlands, of Orange county, N. Y., were famous for woodcock shooting in years gone by, but the birds are now scarce in most of the Eastern states, though a fair number may be bagged in a few localities, and several Southern and Western resorts, particularly the Mississippi bottoms, still afford good sport in summer and autumn.

THE SNIPE.

"But rather seek the plashy swale,
Low in the moist and boggy vale,
Or pass, thro' bushy swamps that hide
With briery hedge the brooklet side."

From Maine to Mexico, and from Connecticut to California, the snipe is a semi-annual visitor, along the marsh-lands bordering on the lakes and rivers. Spring snipe-shooting is legal in many states, but this and summer woodcock shooting should be prohibited—not alone for the preservation of the two species, but to prevent the killing of other game birds, often mere fledglings, met with by the gunners in their rambles.

The snipe, rising with a startled and startling "skaap," and taking a low, zigzag course across the marsh, is a difficult mark for the tyro, but the experienced shooter who is cool and deliberate will readily kill a large proportion of his birds in this line of sport. Snipe-shooting, in autumn, over good dogs, is well worthy of the sportsman's time and attention.

THE SATURDAY BLADE.

You Should Read THE LAST COLUMN On the Last Page of This Paper. IT WILL PAY YOU.

VOL. VII.—NO. 5. CHICAGO, ILL., SATURDAY, JULY 14, 1894. PRICE 5 CENTS.

RIFLES CRACK.

Triggers Pulled by Chicago Militiamen.

Two Men Killed and Many More Injured in the First Real Conflict of the Strike.

Soldiers Attacked by a Dangerous Armed Mob.

GREAT STRIKE

Ordered by Various Labor Leaders.

The Pullman Company Positively Refuses to Arbitrate and the Tie-Up Is Now On.

More Than a Million Men Will Quit Work.

THF FIRST REAL CONFLICT OF THE PULLMAN BOYCOTT.

Troops and Rioters Come Together at Forty-Seventh Street in This City. Deadly Volleys Poured Into the Frenzied Mob With Fatal Results. Several Killed and a Long List of Wounded.

WILL FIGHT

Government's Military Forces in California.

Will Be Met by an Army of Strikers Who Have Secured 1,400 Rifles.

Talk of Martial Law Creates Wildest Excitement.

HAMMOND RIOT.

Bloody Work in the Indiana Suburb.

Mob Takes Possession of the Town Early Sunday Morning and Attacks Pullman Cars.

One Man Killed and Many Wounded by the Regulars.

TWO WOMEN

And One Man Killed by Soldiers at Westville, Ill.

FOES OF PEACE

Are Warned by the President's Proclamation.

The Regular Soldiers Preparing Camp On the Lake Front.

Mob Destroying Railway Property Last Thursday Night.

HOW THE FIGHT COMMENCED.

WIFE MURDER.

WRITES TO CLEVELAND.

BATTLE AT SPRING VALLEY

DOCK-WORKERS ARE KILLED.

POPE'S HEALTH IS GOOD.

SIXTY PASSENGERS DROWNED.

(Continued On Second Page.)

THE CHICAGO LEDGER

A MODERN HOME WEEKLY OF ROMANCE, DEPARTMENTS AND EVENTS

VOLUME XXII, NUMBER 30. | CHICAGO, ILL., WEDNESDAY, JULY 25, 1894—SIXTEEN PAGES | SINGLE COPIES 5 CENTS.

An Escaped Convict or The Plot against Tishie

"As lovely as you are, Miss, I'll strangle you and take them."

AN ESCAPED CONVICT;

OR,

The Plot Against Tishie.

By LEON LEWIS.

CHAPTER V.

"TWO WANDERING VAGRANTS!"

CHAPTER VI.

WITH HER PRETENDED RELATIVES.

CHAPTER VII.

GETTING ACQUAINTED.

CHAPTER VIII.

A FUGITIVE FROM JUSTICE.

Only Results Count

HOROLOGICAL INSTITUTE.—*Our experience with your List has been very satisfactory.*
PARSON IDE & CO., Peoria, Ill.

TELEPHONES.—*Boyce's Big Weeklies pay us better than any papers we use.*
UNITED ELECTRIC TELEPHONE CO., Chicago.

TOBACCO HABIT CURE.—*Boyce's Weeklies have always paid us.*
STERLING REMEDY CO., Indiana Mineral Spring Co.

PIANOS AND ORGANS.—*Your papers are pullers.*
GEO. P. BENT, Chicago.

LIQUOR HABIT CURE.—*We get three times more replies from Boyce's Weeklies than from any papers we use.* GOLDEN SPECIFIC CO., Cincinnati.

BICYCLES.—*We are pleased with your list and increase our space with you.*
ROUSE, HAZARD & CO., Peoria, Ill.

CIRCULATION PROVED WEEKLY

WATCHES AND JEWELRY.—*Boyce's Weeklies always pay us.*
NATIONAL M'FG & IMPORTING CO., Chicago.

PUBLISHERS.—*Boyce's Weeklies beat anything in America in the way of results.* F. D. DRAKE, Chicago.

CIGARS.—*Our test shows Boyce's Weeklies to pull fifteen times better than anything we used.*
SYNDICATE CIGAR FACTORY, Chicago.

PATENTS.—*We find nothing to equal Boyce's Weeklies.*
HOPKINS & ATKINS, Washington, D. C.

TELEPHONES.—*Your List brings more results than anything we use.*
MECHANICAL TELEPHONE CO., Albion, Ill.

TYPEWRITERS.—*Your Weeklies pay us better than anything we have used since we have been in business.*
ODELL TYPEWRITER CO., Chicago.

MUSICAL INSTRUMENTS.—*We show our opinion of Boyce's List by doubling our space this year.*
LYON & HEALY.

500,000 Copies Weekly Proved

RATES—$1.60 per Agate line, per insertion.

RULES—Any advertisement discontinued at any time for any reason. No discount for time or space. Circulation proved by P. O. receipts. Reading notices same rate as display.

THE CHICAGO WORLD.

FOURTH YEAR—NO 29. CHICAGO, ILL., SUNDAY, JULY 22, 1894. PRICE 5 CENTS.

DEBS GOES TO JAIL.

The American Railway Union President and Three Associates are Held for Contempt.

BAMBOOZLED!

The Clever Trick of a Kansas Convict on Governor Lewelling to Secure Freedom.

FRIGHTFUL EXPLOSION OF DYNAMITE IN A COLLIERY AT HAZLETON, PA.

While the Sticks Are Being Distributed to the Miners in the Shaft the Explosion Takes Place, Blowing at Least Fifteen Men to Atoms—The Horrible Scene in the Pit When the Rescuers Entered.

THE OTHER GIRL.

Senator Blackburn of Kentucky Trots Her Out in the Breckinridge Scandal.

LO, ON THE WARPATH.

STOLEN SWEETS

Were So Delightful to Pretty Lilly Fisk That She Easily Yielded to Them.

DEATH IN A MINE.

Two Hundred Sticks of Dynamite Explode in a Colliery at Hazleton, Pa.

THE STRIKE IS OVER.

BIG FUNERAL AT ST. PAUL.

WAS JEALOUS OF THE DEAD.

W. D. Boyce Office Building

112-114 Dearborn Street Chicago

THERE are **one** hun-dred and eighty-six (186) outside rooms in this building. It is finished in marble, mosaic, metal and mahogany, and is the most expensive building, per cubic foot, yet erected in Chicago.

It is headquarters in Chicago for advertising agents, branch offices of out-of-town newspapers, special advertising agents and correspondents. The newspaper fraternity and kindred businesses are largely gathered together here, and save time in transacting business with each other.

The Chicago Newspaper Club occupy the entire fourth floor.

The publishing and printing offices of the BLADE, LEDGER, and WORLD—"Boyce's Big Weeklies"—are **not** located here but at 113-117 Fifth Avenue.

We paid for 52 Weeks ending Sept. 1st, 1894 **$28,228.76** Postage at 1c per lb.

AGENTS' SPECIALTIES.—*Your Weeklies are paying us.*
MONROE ERASER CO., LaCrosse, Wis.

PUBLISHERS.—*Your papers are pullers.*
PASSUMPSIC PUB. CO., Passumpsic, Vt.

CORRESPONDENCE CLUB.—*Our test books show your papers at the top of the ladder.*
CLAUDE MONROE, Clarksburg W. Va.

OBESITY SPECIALIST.—*Boyce's Weeklies pay all the year.* DR. O. W. F. SNYDER, Chicago.

ADVERTISING AGENCY.—*We find Boyce's Weeklies the best mediums we do business with.*
KANSAS CITY AD. CO., Kansas City, Mo.

MEDICAL SPECIALTIES.—*Boyce's Weeklies pay us better than any papers we use.*
W. H. CHIDESTER & SON, New York.

Average Circulation for the year......... **533,549** Copies Weekly

PATENTS.—*We are much pleased with the results we obtain from our ad. in your papers.*
WALTON & CO., Washington, D. C.

BOOKS.—*We find we get better results and more good agents from your Weeklies than any medium we use.*
BEE PUB CO., Chicago.

ADVERTISING AGENCY.—*I pay more money to Boyce's Weeklies than to any newspaper in the country.*
STANLEY DAY, New Market, N. J.

BUGGIES.—*We have used your papers many times. We find no better.* WILBUR H. MURRAY, Cincinnati, O.

MEDICINE.—*We are in receipt daily of a vast number of orders from persons who say they saw our ad. in the Blade, Ledger or World. You have the greatest of the great weeklies.* MURAT MED. CO., Cincinnati, O.

We contracted to prove.............. **500,000** Copies Weekly

We have exceeded our contract by.... **33,549** Copies Weekly

Every year we have shown more circulation than we agreed to. That is a practice we have. Put BOYCE'S BIG WEEKLIES on the list.

Lightning Source UK Ltd.
Milton Keynes UK
UKHW040637250219
337804UK00008B/1430/P